Jess Maltby Malabre.

Jamaica. September 42.

THE SMALLER DEMOCRACIES

by

SIR E. D. SIMON

LONDON
VICTOR GOLLANCZ LTD
1939

PRINTED IN GREAT BRITAIN BY RICHARD CLAY AND COMPANY, LTD. (T.U.)
BUNGAY, SUFFOLK.

PREFACE

I HAVE for years regarded the maintenance and strengthening of democracy as by far the most important and most urgent question in the world. British democracy is so complex and on such a large scale that it is hard to understand clearly the reasons for its strength and its weaknesses. It is difficult to learn much about other democracies from books; I was impressed when I read that Lord Bryce had got 90 per cent. of what he put into that very fine book *Modern Democracies* from personal contacts and 10 per cent. out of books. I decided, therefore, to visit some of the small successful democracies, and found, as Lord Bryce did, that personal contacts with people of all kinds of experience and outlook, living and working in these countries, enabled me in a comparatively short time to get a grasp of their main problems which I could never have got out of books. In any case the books in English on the politics of the Scandinavian countries are most inadequate. My aim has been to seek out what has been done well, in the hope of finding things from which we could draw useful lessons for our own democracy. I have endeavoured not to ignore failures; I may perhaps have drawn an unduly favourable picture on the whole; but surely in these dark days it is permissible to dwell on the brighter side of things.

I have a wide experience of different aspects of the working of democracy in England, as a City Councillor and Lord Mayor of Manchester, as an officer of Manchester University, as a Member of Parliament and for a short time a member of the Government, and as Chairman and Governing Director of two engineering and contracting firms working in Britain and about thirty other countries. In these various capacities I have gained experience which has given me some background against which to try to understand the problems of other countries.

The achievements of some of these small countries are extraordinarily heartening: Switzerland, where Germans, French, and Italians, differing in race, language, and religion, live together in peace and goodwill; Denmark, where 200,000 small farmers have built up a new owner-co-operator system of farming, at once the most democratic and the most efficient in the world; Sweden, which has done more than any country to abolish unemployment and to reconcile the interests of town and country and of capital and labour.

I offer this book in the hope that it may suggest to readers some methods by which things may be improved in England. But I realise how sketchy and inadequate it is, and hope that it may be possible to follow it up by a series of books dealing much more fully with the problems, the failures, and still more the successes of the small democracies in the world.

ACKNOWLEDGMENTS

I owe my warmest thanks to literally hundreds of people, from the muleteer who received us in Lötschental to the President of the Swiss Republic and the Prime Ministers of Sweden and Denmark, to men and women of every kind of experience and occupation and opinion who had only two things in common: their love of democracy and their friendly willingness to answer my endless questions. I owe my thanks in particular to a number of my friends in each country who have been good enough to read through my descriptive chapters: all these chapters have been read and criticised by people of different experience and opinions. Even so, I alone am responsible for them; the last three chapters of conclusions are still more wholly my own responsibility, as I have not had time or opportunity to get expert criticism of these.

ACKNOWLEDGMENTS

I owe my warmest thanks to literally hundreds of people, from the ministers who received me in Düsseldorf, to the President of the Swiss Republic and the Prime Ministers of Sweden and Denmark, to men and women of every kind of experience and occupation and opinion who had only two things in common: their love of democracy and their friendly willingness to answer my endless questions. I owe my thanks in particular to a number of my friends in each country who have been good enough to read through my descriptive chapters; all these chapters have been read and criticised by people of different experience and opinions. Even so, I alone am responsible for them; the last three chapters of conclusions are still more wholly my own responsibility, as I have not had time or opportunity to get expert criticism of these.

CONTENTS

A 2

CONTENTS

CHAPTER I

THE CHALLENGE TO DEMOCRACY

We are to-day in the midst of one of the greatest crises of civilisation. A wave of barbarism is sweeping over the world, unparalleled in history, threatening to destroy everything that is best in human society. Are men to live as free citizens of democracies, or are they to be docile followers of a despot, forced to develop the servile mass mentality which dictators demand from their subjects? That is beyond all comparison the greatest issue which faces mankind to-day.

The dictators hate and despise all the values which are the aim of democrats—peace and freedom and justice, kindliness and love of truth.

The challenge to democracy is summarised in the words of Mussolini, with which he has plastered the walls of Italy for the last two years: " Believe, Obey, Fight ", and in his sayings :—

" Words are beautiful things. Machine-guns, ships, aeroplanes, are still more beautiful."

" War alone brings to its highest tension all human energy and puts the stamp of nobility on the people who have courage to lead it."

And by Hitler as follows :—

" Death in the battlefield should be looked on as a longed-for conclusion of life."

" In everlasting battle mankind has achieved greatness; in everlasting peace it would be doomed to destruction."

What can we do to maintain and strengthen democracy in face of this terrific challenge?

One of the first things is to try to understand it. We in England have enjoyed liberty and security for so long that we assume them as a matter of course, and forget that " the price of liberty is eternal vigilance ".

Those of us who try to understand democracy generally

think about our own country. Some tend to think of our failures: the economic injustice of the whole system, the idle rich living in luxury, the poverty and misery of the slums; the tragic failure to find work for nearly two million unemployed, the slow demoralisation of those who feel they are not wanted because they have no job and no part in the life of the country; the fact that we seem to have lost the art of government and leadership, that our foreign policy is so flabby and weak that we are losing our influence in the world, that no useful action is being taken to deal with the scandal of the depressed areas, that in spite of the malnutrition of large numbers of children, milk for children is so expensive that the unemployed cannot afford it at all, while immense quantities of surplus milk are being sold for manufacturing purposes at a quarter the price at which the unemployed can buy it.

Others tend to think of what is good in our democracy: the age-long growth of freedom in Britain; the founding of the Empire, a model for the League of Nations, preserving peace among four hundred million people of many races, creeds, and colours; uniting Britain with the free and equal self-governing Dominions under the crown; of the humanitarian movement of the last 150 years, which has revolutionised the condition of prisoners, of lunatics, of the feeble-minded, of the poor and unfortunate, and above all of the children; of the great system of social reform built up mainly in the last generation, the services for health and education, old-age pensions, poor and unemployment relief, and social insurance; of England's great achievement in building since the war three and a half million houses, well planned, well built, each standing in its own garden, housing over a third of the population—a far greater housing achievement than that of any totalitarian state.

Each of these views is one-sided. Immense tasks lie before us; but most of us believe that even to-day Britain offers at least as good a life to the average person as any of the great countries in the world. We believe that the totalitarian ideals, though superficially attractive to youth, are in fact the deadly enemies of the welfare and progress of mankind, that the only road to a finer future lies through the free use of human reason by the mass of men, that kindliness and freedom and social responsibility, which offer unlimited possibilities for the development of a better and nobler life for men, are the things most worth preserving in the world and that they are only possible under some form of democracy.

Democracy cannot succeed, however, unless its citizens co-operate in working for their own ideals with at least the same belief in them, with the same courage and zeal as that shown by the subjects of the dictators. Since democracy in a large country like England is a most complex thing, we must try to understand it more clearly than most of us do now before we can hope to believe in it whole-heartedly. We must, therefore, try to answer such fundamental questions as the following:—

What do we mean by democracy?

Why do we believe in it?

What are the achievements of democracy? Can it provide peace and security and the opportunity of a good life for its citizens? In particular, can it abolish unemployment and poverty?

What are the characteristics of the good citizen of democracy?

What political institutions are necessary to effective democracy?

What are the underlying conditions which cause countries to become democracies and to succeed in establishing good standards of living for the people?

In the following chapters I have attempted to find answers to some of these questions, not out of my own consciousness nor by a study of the ancient philosophers; not by a study of the great democracies, England, France and the United States, where conditions are so complex as to be hard to understand, but by examining the working of democracy in certain small countries where it is successful and where the problems are much simpler. The five countries which I have investigated—Switzerland, Sweden, Denmark, Norway, and Finland—have been chosen largely for reasons of convenience; it is not suggested that their democracy is more successful than that in the British Dominions, Belgium, or Holland. My conclusions as to what can be learnt from these democracies will be found in the last chapters.

CHAPTER II

SOME ASPECTS OF SWISS DEMOCRACY

MOST thoughtful Swiss people regard the experience acquired by the citizens in the small self-governing communes as the very basis of the remarkable success of Swiss democracy.[1] Most of the communes are very small; their powers vary from canton to canton, but on the average seem to be about equal to those of an English county borough, with the one conspicuous difference that the communes have from time immemorial had the right to purchase and own land, a right of which very wide advantage has been taken.

The story of the communes has been much neglected in such books on Switzerland as I have been able to discover. I have, therefore, concentrated on local government in the communes, while dealing very sketchily with the cantons and the state, which are far better known and were admirably dealt with in Lord Bryce's great book on *Modern Democracies*.

The success of Swiss democracy is political rather than economic. It is true that their agriculture is efficient, that they have succeeded in building up a surprisingly powerful engineering industry, and that, of course, the tourist industry is important, but the classic achievement of the Swiss is their success in creating a strong unified state consisting of Germans, French, and Italians, speaking different languages and having different religions. They have, of course, to deal with the inevitable problems of the relations of town and country and of capital and labour, and on the whole these are being fairly successfully handled. But added to these they have their tremendous problems of racial and religious differences. An examination of the

[1] Switzerland has a population of about four million, divided into more than 3,000 communes with an average population of about 1,300.

political working of the communes throws some light on their national democratic achievement. I have, therefore, devoted myself mainly to examining the constitution and the working of certain communes, varying from Blatten, with a population of 340, to Zurich, with a population almost a thousand times as great.

In particular, I have dealt fully with the village of Blatten in the valley of Lötschental, as it is an almost perfect example of a primitive and conservative democracy working on a very small scale with the most remarkable degree of success.

LÖTSCHENTAL

Lötschental is a narrow and most lovely valley, about ten miles long to the farthest inhabited part. It runs east and west between two ranges of high snow mountains, impassable except to mountaineers. Till the last generation, the only access was up a steep path from the Rhône Valley. It is said that of old the whole of the imports for the thousand persons living in the valley were brought in on the back of one mule once a year!

Recently a railway has been built to Goppenstein (4,000 feet) at the west end of the valley, and a road has been made three miles eastwards along the valley. There are several small villages. For administrative purposes the valley is divided into four communes. The farthest village is Blatten, which lies 5,000 feet above the sea; it has a population of 340 out of a total valley population to-day of 1,200.

During the last thirty years tourists have begun to frequent Lötschental, and a few small hotels have been built. Their money has helped somewhat to raise the standard of living of the peasants, but has so far not seriously affected the lives of the people.

The peasants have to contend with severe natural difficulties. For six months of the year the whole valley is under snow. During summer the weather is so dry that artificial irrigation is necessary for all the fields. There is very little level land, so that agriculture is carried on under great difficulties. But the most grievous harm is caused by avalanches. Bridges, dams, roads, and fields are constantly damaged. There are so few spots which are not liable to avalanche that the villages have to be crowded closely together on the safe parts; so much so that only narrow spaces are allowed between the houses and farm buildings. The paths are dirty and often soaked in manure. The whole arrangement is most insanitary.

To show the power of the avalanches two examples may be given. In the spring of 1937 a whole village of thirty-five buildings situated on one of the higher grazing lands in Blatten was totally destroyed by an avalanche. The owners are now busily at work rebuilding, a very heavy drain indeed on their time and resources. It is interesting to note that the canton offered a subsidy of 60 per cent. to erect a single large building on another site, but the peasants felt that they could not afford this, and having regard to the fact that it was 160 years since the same village had been destroyed by an avalanche they decided to rebuild on the same site.

The manager of the very pleasant hotel at the top of the valley told us that he had stocked the three small lakes in the neighbourhood with trout, but in all three cases avalanches had swept out the lakes and killed every fish.

Beliefs : Religious, Political, Economic

The residents in the valley belong to the Roman Catholic Church and the Catholic Conservative Party. The priest boasts that every single one of the 400 voters in Lötschental invariably votes for that party.

Everybody shares these faiths, everybody regards them as the only basis of a good life. Every leader, whether priest or teacher or politician, inculcates them continually and automatically. All the varied ceremonies—drama, singing, processions, and the constant wearing on Sundays and holidays of the ancient local costume—tend to maintain and strengthen the old customs, traditions, and beliefs. The old priest, spiritual leader and lover of the valley, believes in its future mainly for two reasons: first, the costume, evidence of adherence to the good customs of the past (he relates with pride that his mother wore her special valley hat all her life, indoors and out); and second, the single political party, which prevents jealousy and faction and " dangerous thoughts ". His authority is unquestioned in religious matters, and seems to be considerable in politics, though officially he does not intervene. But he said " We do not invite into our valley political speakers who seem to us to hold the wrong views ". Disturbing ideas seem to be effectively excluded: the radio is hardly known; a cinema show is a rare occurrence; nearly everybody reads the local Catholic-Conservative paper. Those who leave the valley and return seem to accept the local customs as fully as those who have never left it.

Economically there seems to be no desire to change. Every peasant owns his own land, buildings, and stock. There are no rich residents; the priest and schoolmaster are no better off than the "rich" peasant; and he only owns half a dozen cattle. There is no unemployment, little serious poverty, no exploitation; the peasants not only know, but themselves determine exactly how their taxes shall be spent.

The peasants are poor, but live a varied and interesting and friendly life. They are proud of the beauties of their valley; proud of their independence, which is such that people talk of the " Canton Lötschental ".[1] Every citizen is a self-respecting man living his life in security, his firm faith in his religion and in his political party untouched by modern doubts. " Nerves " are unknown, quarrels, of course, occur but rarely last a fortnight. Progress is exceedingly slow. It is a conservative civilisation and wishes to remain so. In spite of increasing tourist traffic, in spite of all the inventions of modern science, the valley is still almost as securely protected from disturbing thoughts as it was 500 years ago.

BLATTEN

Agriculture and Economics

The valley lives by agriculture; there are no factories. There is a small area of good land at the bottom of the valley; there are patches of grazing land on the hillsides known as "Alps", and there is, of course, a considerable area of forest.

[1] The canton being an almost completely self-governing unit, with power of life and death over its citizens.

The valley is divided into four communes, Blatten the largest being situated at the top end of the valley.

The population of Blatten is about 340 including 110 men of twenty years or over, all of whom are Swiss citizens and voters.

The priest informed us that between 1714 and 1914 christenings in Lötschental had exceeded burials by 1,200. There must have been about six emigrants from the valley each year.

The women play no public part in the valley. Their time is fully occupied looking after their houses and their children, helping on the land, spinning and weaving and making clothes both for themselves and the men. On holidays and on Sundays they still almost invariably wear the traditional costume, and the priest informed us that this would certainly not be changed so long as he was alive.

When we were passing through the village, just after Mass on a Sunday morning, we found most of the male population listening to a visiting band; there was not one single woman. When we asked the reason, we were told, with an air of surprise at our question, that " naturally " every woman wanted not to amuse herself but to go home and cook the Sunday dinner.

The houses nearly all consist of two living-rooms, a kitchen, and an attic. The average floor area of the more modern houses is about 700 square feet, about the same as the average post-war municipal house in England. There is electric light in most of the houses; water is laid on to a considerable number. There are on the average about seven persons per house. It is generally possible to separate the sexes in the bedrooms by using both rooms and the attic for sleeping purposes.

A house of this sort costs about £1,000, an astonishingly high figure—well over double what a similar house would cost in England. Housing seems to be expensive throughout Switzerland, and, of course, the cost of transport in Lötschental is exceedingly heavy.

Each peasant has also a simple house on the grazing alp and various farm buildings, cow-sheds, hay barns, food stores, scattered about in the village, on the fields, and in the alps. Owing to the heavy cost of transport, which is possible only on the backs of mules or of men or women, it is necessary to have a large amount of storage in different places, so as to reduce to the minimum the transport of hay, manure, and milk by storing and consuming the hay and manure as near as possible to where it is produced.

The amount of good land owned by each peasant varies from about one to four acres, and is said to be split up on the average into no less than seventy-one small plots! The peasants own on the average two and a half cows, five sheep, two goats, and half a pig. The great bulk of the land is under grass for hay or pasture, but in the tiny arable plots they grow their own potatoes and a good deal of rye.

The only way in which the peasants get money is by the sale of a cow or calf and a certain amount of butter; these sales have to pay for the whole of the imports into the valley.

The standard of living is, of course, exceedingly low, but it is a good deal better than it was thirty years ago. No fruit grows in the valley, and last year there was considerable import of apples. Coffee is also now widely drunk as against the buttermilk which was almost universally drunk thirty years ago. Practically nothing is spent on alcohol, because they have not the necessary money.

The only people in the village who have salaries are the postmaster, the priest who gets 3,000 francs a year and sixty kilos of butter, the teacher who gets 3,000 francs for six month's teaching and usually works on the land in the summer. There are three or four who live by trading, shopkeepers, and an innkeeper (dependent on tourists); nine of the peasants are guides and about seven own mules and live by transport.

Democracy

The commune is governed by the communal Assembly which consists of all the male citizens of twenty and over, of whom there are 110. The Assembly elects an executive of five persons, including a president and a vice-president, for periods of four years. The executive is responsible for all routine administration, and calls the Assembly together whenever it considers it necessary. The Assembly usually meets after Mass at 11 o'clock on Sunday mornings. All matters involving an expenditure of over 1,000 francs must be submitted to the Assembly; in practice everything of any importance is put before them, so that every voter in the village has an opportunity of hearing about and helping to take a decision on all matters of any moment.

The executive nominates a considerable number of committees, each consisting normally of a president and two other members. The principal work carried out by the executive and the committees is as follows.

Finance.

The finance committee, under the treasurer, assesses the property and income of each resident, fixes the amount of the local tax, and collects the taxes. The president showed me his annual financial report, excellently arranged and very neatly written. It is read over to the municipal Assembly, which takes about an hour, and then discussed and, as he told me, generally approved with little trouble. Only an educated and competent person could keep these fairly complicated accounts in order. The keeping of them and the collection of the taxes must take a very considerable amount of time.

Justice.

There is no whole-time or uniformed policeman, no prison or lock-up. The community is so well-behaved that nothing of the sort is found to be necessary. But the head of the committee of justice has the power of temporary arrest pending the calling in of a policeman from the canton.

Fire Prevention.

The danger of fire with the closely crowded wooden houses is great. The fire-prevention committee inspects every house four times a year and makes sure that it conforms with the regulations. Any faults are reported to the municipal Assembly. This is again voluntary unpaid work.

About half the citizens are trained to deal with outbreaks of fire, and the time spent in training is paid for at the rate of 50 centimes an hour. Thanks to their precautions, there has been no serious fire in the valley since about 1900, when one of the villages was completely burnt to the ground owing to an outbreak of fire occurring while the whole population was at Mass.

Poor Relief.

There is no unemployment; poverty and misfortune are normally looked after by the family, which plays a very important part in local life. The committee has mainly to deal with orphans and sometimes with people who have left the valley and returned in unfortunate circumstances. They have never had to relieve adult permanent residents.

Public Works.

This is one of the main committees having to deal with the making and maintenance of paths, bridges, water supply, and electric power (they have their own hydro-electric station).

The biggest problem at present before the commune is the question of extending the existing road by about three miles from the lower part of the valley up to Blatten.

The existing road was built in 1920; each of the four communes contributed and Blatten's share was 60,000 francs the whole of which still stands as a debt in the accounts.

The canton and the Bund have now offered to pay grants of 45 per cent. each to extend the road to Blatten. There has been an interesting controversy in the matter. In the first place, the lower villages who already have the road are now by no means anxious to pay their share towards extending the road up the valley. They think this will take the tourist traffic past them and actually damage them. There is further opposition from the seven Blatten residents who make their living by mule transport and who would be ruined if motor-cars were allowed up to Blatten. On the other hand the average resident of Blatten expects benefits owing to the reduced cost of transport, and the hotel-keepers in Blatten would naturally benefit most of all.

Blatten has therefore its " pressure groups ", the rich hotel-keepers wanting the road, the muleteers opposing it. But the motives of each group are perfectly well known to every voter; the hotel-keepers would never think of using their money power, nor in fact would they be able to do so, owing to the honesty of the people and the fact that such transactions could hardly be kept secret; so that the

different interests are freely open to work for their own
aims. There is no danger in Lötschental of the serious
distortion of public opinion, which is often caused by rich
pressure groups in large democracies like England or
America.

Health.

There is no drainage; manure lies in heaps all round the
closely crowded houses. The general view is that it has
always been so, that nothing else can be done, and that it
is not really unhealthy. There is a " Sick Association "
to which each member pays three francs a year; about
90 per cent. of the residents in the valley belong to it.
With the help of this money and a substantial subsidy
from the canton there is a resident doctor whose services
and medicine are given free. Apart from this little is done
in an organised way for the health of the community.

Education.

There are about twenty-five boys and the same number of
girls who are taught in separate schools, by a man and a
woman teacher respectively.

The boys' school occupies the ground floor of a building
belonging to the commune, the upper floor being used
mainly for meetings of the municipal Assembly. The
school consists of a small lobby, with pegs for clothes, and a
room fitted with desks and the minimum of necessary
furniture for the twenty-five boys. It is heated by
electricity. It would be difficult to imagine anything more
primitive and cheap, though it is warm and dry. Some of
the children have to walk half an hour to get to school.
The teacher says that their health is good and the average
attendance high. The commune pays towards the teachers'
salaries a capital tax of one-tenth of 1 per cent. which
amounts to 1,000 francs. The canton adds 2,000, making
the salary for each of the two teachers 3,000 francs (for
six months' work). The canton sends an inspector early
in the school year and again at the end of the year to
conduct an examination.

The school year consists of six months' continuous work
during the winter and six months' holiday. It is an eight-
year course from the age of seven to fifteen, followed by a

compulsory continuation course of 120 hours a year for
four years. This includes twenty hours of religion given
by the priest; of the rest, given by the teacher, history,
law, and citizenship are major subjects.

The one teacher is thus responsible for teaching the
children for twelve years. Each year he has about three
new boys who stay with him from the age of about seven
to nineteen. The priest told us that this system, which,
of course, prevails only in remote rural areas, gave excellent
results. The six months' work with the family during the
summer, on the land and in the house, gives them practical
experience, teaches them responsibility, and is admirable
from the health point of view. The six months' steady
intellectual work during the winter prepares them for
examinations so well that they can hold their own with the
children from the towns. This must naturally depend on
the quality of the teacher. The teacher at Blatten who has
for the last ten years been president of the commune, is a
man of high quality, and no doubt capable of carrying this
very heavy responsibility effectively. When I asked him
how many of the citizens of Blatten would be able to keep
the somewhat elaborate accounts of the commune in order,
he said that in his opinion the majority could certainly
reach this pretty high standard successfully.

" Burger " Assembly (Bürgergemeinde).

Nearly all the forest land in the commune, as well as a
little grazing land, belongs to the so-called " Burger "
Assembly. Membership has to be gained by inheritance
or by purchase. All the sons of a burger are automatically
qualified. Membership gives rights to timber, mainly
for purposes of firewood, and involves duties to maintain
the forests and other land. Every year on Whit-Sunday
the burgers meet together for a feast and merry-making;
also they meet occasionally as a body to decide what is
to be done about the forests. Every year the members
spend about two days in large groups clearing the forest,
cutting and carrying the hay—without remuneration.

The routine administration, which is not heavy, is carried
out by a president and two other elected members; it is
interesting to note that the present president is only thirty-
two years of age. He is a guide, a captain in the Swiss

Army, and an inn-keeper. He is a man of considerable qualities; for instance, he is perturbed that the forests have been going backward in recent years, and is trying hard to develop a scheme of afforestation. As an instance of the economical administration of the affairs of Blatten, he told us that he has several times met the expert forester of the canton and occasionally had to entertain him to lunch. Not only has he been allowed no expenses, but he has paid for the forester's lunch himself.

The canton is offering a 50 per cent. grant towards an afforestation scheme. But the poverty of the citizens is such that they can only provide their share by unpaid labour, on which there will, of course, be no return for twenty years. Yet he hopes to get the scheme through. This indicates a fine public spirit. I wonder what the citizens of Manchester would say if they were asked to give two days a year of free labour towards the afforestation of their water-works?

There are only two residents in Blatten who have not the rights of citizenship. They are granted these rights and duties from year to year for an annual payment of 75 francs.

The Grazing Co-operative.

The various grazing alps on the hillside have from time immemorial been owned co-operatively by a number of peasants; every peasant belongs to one of these groups. The co-operative as a whole has grazing land for a certain number of cattle. Each individual peasant may have the right to graze anything from one-quarter of a cow up to say five cows. Each peasant has part or the whole of a simple house and cow-shed. The agricultural operations are rather complicated, but broadly speaking the cows are grazed for about two months in the summer and sometimes also in the autumn. During the summer the cows are milked and looked after generally by the women; often the women and children spend two pleasant months of what is practically a summer holiday on the alp.

The management of the alp is in the hands of the whole of the peasant owners, who meet early in June to discuss arrangements for the year and spend generally about two days as a group clearing up the winter damage and preparing the alp for its year's work—each peasant, rich or poor, spends the same amount of time in this common work; again without remuneration.

Relations with the Canton.

The canton plays a considerable part in the life of the commune by way of supervision and subsidy. We have already shown that it pays two-thirds of the salaries of the teachers and inspects the education. It has a professional forester to advise the commune and strictly controls all cutting down of trees. It is prepared to subsidise a proper scheme of afforestation. The canton and the Bund are offering a large subsidy for the new road, and the canton occasionally offers grants for rebuilding after disasters due to avalanche. There are other small subsidies as, for instance, one towards the expenses of a midwife. But on the whole it can fairly be said that as regards local self-government the bulk of the responsibility falls on the commune itself.

Cantonal or national politics play only a small part in the life of the commune. The members are such unanimous and whole-hearted supporters of the Catholic Conservative Party that serious discussion of the larger aspects of politics seems to be rare; though on occasions there may be a good deal of discussion on some important referendum.

The Education of the Citizen.

Let us consider how far the education and experience of the citizen of Blatten enable him to judge wisely of measures and of men; for this is probably the best test of the efficient working of a democracy.

Practically every peasant is a member of three bodies:—

> The communal Assembly;
> The " Burger " Assembly;
> A grazing co-operative.

The communal Assembly is the governing body of the commune; all matters of any importance come before it. As a member, the peasant not only knows everything that is being done, how almost every franc raised by the taxes is being spent, but personally helps to take every decision.

The " Burger " Assembly and the various grazing co-operatives between them control the whole of the public forests and grazing lands. Each peasant takes part in their various meetings and decisions; and each peasant has to put in three or four days' free work in the year repairing the damage of the winter and doing the many jobs which are necessary to put the land into good working order.

Every peasant, therefore, spends a considerable amount of time on the ordinary business of democracy: discussing and making decisions on public affairs. Meetings of the whole of the citizens are held perhaps on twenty Sundays each year to vote on national or cantonal affairs, or to deal with the affairs of the commune. The attendance varies from 50 to 90 per cent., according to the importance of the agenda. In this way every citizen acquires the habits of discussion and persuasion, of reaching agreement, of the good-humoured acceptance of the decision of the majority, which is so fundamental to the effective working of democracy.

Further, every citizen spends several days in the year actually doing work with his own hands for the public benefit. If that work is done less strenuously than the work on his own plot, if there is something of a holiday atmosphere in this public co-operative work, that is no bad thing. The work is done and done voluntarily by the whole of the peasants, equally by the rich and the poor, without any pay.

But apart from all this experience of public work in which every inhabitant plays his part, those who have any capacity for public leadership do far more; for almost the whole administration of the affairs of the commune is done voluntarily by unpaid leaders. There are about forty administrative posts, divided at any one time between about twenty-five citizens. They administer the finances, including the preparation of the budget and of the annual accounts, the assessing and collection of the taxes, the police, fire brigade, education, health, relief of poverty, control of roads, paths and bridges, irrigation, hydro-electric plant, and many other things; in fact the whole of the complex work necessary for carrying on even so small and simple a community as Blatten.

Occasionally, where the work takes a man away from

his own job for half a day or more, he is paid at the fixed rate of fifty centimes per hour. Last year the amount so paid amounted to a total of 160 francs; surely the cheapest administration in the world!

The president is the school teacher; he was elected at the surprisingly young age of twenty-four, and is now serving his third four-year term of office. He lives in the same type of house as the peasants, and is in the closest possible touch with them. Educated in the local school, he went for three years to the cantonal Teachers' Training College. He has general control of the administration; he himself keeps the main accounts, which are somewhat complicated, in the most perfect order. I had long discussions with him, and was much impressed by his public spirit, his common sense, and his ability. He would certainly be an outstanding member of the Manchester City Council.

None of the other four members of the executive is over forty years of age; it has in recent years been the custom in Blatten to elect young men to office, which they usually hold for two periods, or eight years. Generally they then retire, having done their share, and remain as ordinary, but experienced members of the communal Assembly. Not less than half the citizens have passed through the executive, and have, therefore, held responsible office.

The Assembly must be one of the best-informed and most responsible electorates in the world. A potential leader is tried out in some small job; his work is critically watched; if well done he is gradually promoted. There is no hope for the tub-thumper. A candidate is judged, not by oratory, but by his personal character and practical work.

On the other hand, it seems to be the invariable rule that those who are capable of leadership are willing to give the necessary time and thought to the work at least for a period of years. It would seem that the problem of selecting the best leaders in a democracy is solved so far as Blatten is concerned.

There can be no doubt whatever that democracy works well in Blatten. The whole civilisation is stable, people do not move, ideas do not change. The people know one another intimately; the problems are simple. Blatten offers a unique example of a small, stable, and simple community, carrying on its affairs by the most completely democratic methods.   Under these conditions, the voters of Blatten do undoubtedly judge wisely of men and measures, in a way which is utterly impossible in a modern industrial city with a million inhabitants.

MURG

This is a small commune on the Wallensee with about 1,000 inhabitants; roughly 80 per cent. are Roman Catholics, and 20 per cent. Protestants. I happened to arrive there on the day of a Catholic holiday. The President informed me that the Catholics and Protestants were the best of friends, that the Protestants always joined in the celebration of the Catholic holidays, and vice-versa. This arrangement seemed entirely satisfactory to both parties! I was informed that in certain cantons the Protestants and Catholics actually use the same church, the necessary alterations between the services being made by means of screens.

KÖLLIKEN

This is a commune of about 2,400 inhabitants in Canton Aargau, mainly agricultural, but containing a number of small factories. The usual communal meetings are held about three times a year. I attended a meeting at eight o'clock on a weekday evening. Attendance is compulsory for every citizen; two francs fine being imposed for absence. The great bulk of those who attended were peasants. They came informally in their working clothes, some wearing caps, not one in five wore a tie. No woman has ever attended.

Three separate meetings were held one after another; firstly, the Political Assembly, which deals with the usual local authority affairs; secondly, the Church Assembly, which deals with the affairs of the Protestant Church (the great bulk of the inhabitants are Protestants); thirdly, the Burger Assembly, which deals mainly with the considerable area of property owned by the burgers. The membership of the Church and Burger Assemblies is substantially smaller than that of the Political Assembly.   In all three meetings the procedure is similar.   There is an executive of five elected for three years by the whole body; there is also a financial advisory committee, separately elected by the whole body, which reports to the Assembly on all proposals of the Executive, and also reports on the annual report of the Executive. The political executive has a regular weekly meeting, as well as many special meetings. The members are paid about 600 francs a year; the president receives 1,500 francs. The secretary receives a full-time salary of 4,500 francs.

The Political Assembly

The chairman was a small business man, aged about fifty, who handled the business excellently.

There were 400 present. The minutes of the last meeting took twenty minutes to read. There was general conversation which the chairman made no attempt to stop.

Then came the report on the annual accounts, which was presented by the financial adviser, who made a clear and simple statement and offered opportunities for discussion which were not accepted. The Executive then retired. In their absence the meeting approved their report unanimously. The Executive returned; nobody suggested any thanks to them! There was no clapping or other expression of approval or disapproval throughout the whole meeting.

Three proposals were brought before the meeting, the most important being the extension of a main drain. This was introduced in a good ten minutes' speech by the chairman; there were four speeches from the floor, lasting about one minute each, and the report was approved.

The chairman then reported a petition from the midwives of the commune protesting against the new habit of women going to the hospital at Aarau to have their children, and so throwing the midwives out of work. The Executive recommended no action. Approved without discussion.

The Church Assembly

Ten per cent. of those present (mainly Catholics) retired. Procedure exactly similar. The chairman then announced that the priest was retiring. His house was 200 years old. It was necessary to build a new house or go in for heavy repairs. At this point there was a sigh or groan from the audience—the only expression of feeling during the whole evening. The chairman made a ten minutes' speech, saying among other things that he had a report from an architect outside the canton so as to be sure of impartiality, and gave details of repairs required at about £1,000. He asked permission to get formal tenders for the next meeting. Agreed without discussion.

The Burger Assembly

Same procedure. The minutes of the last meeting recorded a long discussion on the question of admitting a rich German family, who had lived twenty years in Kölliken, as burgers. Finally decided by a vote of two to one to admit them, and again by two to one to charge them for the privilege 4,000 francs rather than 3,000 francs.

It was reported that a burger had applied for permission to build a shop on communal land. The burger in question and his relatives retired from the room. The president, in a five minutes' speech, gave the reasons why the Executive advised against this course. There were six speeches from the floor, none over one and a half minutes, mainly in favour of granting the request. There was then a vote, taken as usual by asking the members to stand up. There was an absolute majority of the burgers in favour of granting the request against the advice of the Executive. This was accepted with no comment, no signs of feeling whatever. It is quite understood that the Executive may be occasionally defeated, and this in no wise alters the confidence of the people in them.

Conclusion

The whole business is most informal. The chairman sits throughout the meeting. It is also most businesslike. There were about twenty speeches altogether, none except those of the chairman exceeding about one minute. No points of order, no attempt at oratory for own or party advantage. Everybody said what he had to say quite shortly and generally simply and clearly. Nobody was thanked for anything. I should say that it was a good deal more strictly businesslike than the ordinary annual meeting of the shareholders of a British company.

AARAU

Communal meeting—June 27th, 1938

Aarau is the capital of Canton Aargau, a well-to-do and very pleasant town of 12,000 inhabitants. It is governed by a meeting of the whole of the adult male citizens, who generally meet twice a year. I attended a meeting on June 27th. So far as is known I am the first outsider ever to have attended such a meeting.

For the proceedings to be legal it is necessary for a majority of the voters to attend. After counting the attendance the president announced that there were 3,439 voters. 286 who are over sixty years of age are not compelled to vote, leaving a compulsory vote of 3,118. Of these an absolute majority, or 1,560, are necessary to make the meeting legal. Number present 1,701; or 55 per cent. A small attendance in view of the fact that it is supposed to be compulsory and that a two francs' fine is levied for absence.

The meeting was held in a large, crowded hall, at 5 p.m. on a hot June day. The doors were locked and no one was allowed out till the meeting was finished at about 7 o'clock.

The constitution is as follows:—

The Political Assembly meets usually twice a year. It elects the following bodies:—

1. *An Executive of Seven.* Six of these belong to middle-class parties; one is a Socialist (there has been a Socialist member since 1905). The president, a lawyer, is a whole-time official receiving £600 per annum; the other six receive 2,000 francs each for part-time work They are elected by the Political Assembly for four years individually (not by proportional representation). A recent president continued to serve for a period of twenty-five years and was a very important factor in the administration of the town.

2. *Financial Advisory Committee.* This again is a committee of nine (including two Socialists) separately elected by the Political Assembly. It is responsible for auditing and reporting on the annual accounts which are presented by the Executive. The chairman reports verbally to the

Political Assembly on all proposals made by the Executive. He is a very important person.

3. Small committees are elected for many of the usual services, finance, health, education, public works, electricity, etc. They are appointed partly by the Political Assembly, partly by the Executive. They are consulted by and report to the Executive, who report any disagreement to the Political Assembly.

For the meeting on June 27th a typed agenda of seven items had been circulated. In support of six of the items separate printed documents were circulated, roughly of about 1,000 words each, giving the necessary information. Each of these items was introduced, not by the president of the Executive, but by the chairman of the Financial Advisory Committee. As it happened, his committee was in full agreement with the Executive on all the matters brought forward. He made speeches of varying length up to fifteen minutes on each of these matters. Most of them were ordinary public works matters. One was an interesting proposal to give a grant of £7,000 towards the cost of a cantonal library to be built in Aarau at a total cost of £37,000. There was a full record of the bargaining between the commune and the canton as to the amount of subsidy, the amount of local labour to be employed, the site, and the type of building. The financial adviser also stressed the advantages to Aarau from the cultural and town-planning point of view. This heavy subsidy was unanimously passed without discussion.

There were only three speeches from the floor of the house during the passing of these items on points of no great importance. They were dealt with firmly, but very tactfully, by the president.

The Socialist leader then rose to propose a public works programme. He pointed out that there were 140 unemployed in Aarau, and suggested various items of expenditure to give employment, especially a new bridge over the river. He spoke from the floor, in his shirt sleeves; the usual Socialist speech, but different from the English custom in being delivered on purely business lines, and in the fact that there was not a single manifestation of approval or disapproval during the speech or at the end of it. The chairman replied in an admirable ten minutes' statement of the whole position, technical and financial, as regards the bridge, and the matter was by unanimous consent deferred till the next meeting.

A very experienced teacher who has lived in Aarau for ten years and attended all the meetings, and who takes an active interest in public affairs, gave me the following opinion.

When he first came to Aarau he was under the impression that direct democracy for so large a town was out of date and should be abolished. He had now changed his mind. He was sure that the custom of getting the great bulk of the people together to listen to serious statements and discussion on all the main matters of local government had an educational effect that was invaluable, both in enabling them to understand and make sensible judgments and in giving them a sense of responsibility. He was strongly of opinion that the decisions taken by the Assembly were at least as good, and probably better, than those that would be taken by a small elected council. The leadership was excellent. The best people were willing to serve and were in fact elected to the various committees.

A few years ago he thought there was some sign of boredom among the mass of the citizens at having to attend these meetings. Now, owing to the dictatorships abroad, there was more conscious pride in the old free institutions of Switzerland. (One sign of this was that for the first time at the meeting I attended a good deal of the speaking was in Swiss dialect rather than, as in the past, in German.)

He was of the opinion that the constitution, so apparently cumbrous, worked well; party only appeared during the election. There was general agreement that the government of the city was honest and efficient.

ZURICH

Zurich is the largest town in Switzerland, with a population of 320,000. It is the capital of the Canton of Zurich, which has a population of 650,000.

B

Zurich is the centre of Swiss industry and commerce and is probably not only the largest but the richest town in Switzerland.

In a town of this size government by a general assembly of all the citizens is, of course, out of the question. It is interesting to consider how Swiss democracy has adapted itself to this problem of the government of a relatively large city. How far has it been successful in combining the Swiss traditions of the responsibility of the individual citizen for the government of his town with efficient administration?

In the first place, nature has been kind to Zurich. The town lies at the end of a lake, between two ranges of mountains; two beautiful rivers flow through the centre of the town, which is surrounded by fields and forests; the climate is pleasant both in summer and winter.

Those who have built the town in the past have taken good advantage of these natural opportunities. It is on the whole well planned and well built. The buildings generally are well designed and well arranged. Even the slums are picturesque.

The works are scattered throughout the town. The power used is entirely electric, and many of the factories are even heated to a large extent by surplus electricity. For an industrial town Zurich is almost unbelievably free from smoke and grit.

The area of Zurich is about 20,000 acres, of which about 30 per cent. consists of open spaces. There are many pleasant woods, which belong to the city, both inside the city area and just outside.

While the town is situated at the end of the lake, there are villages right along both sides of the lake for a distance of over ten miles, all of which are practically suburbs of Zurich though mostly not included in the city area.

The city has several very attractive residential quarters for the well-to-do, generally with fine views over the lake and hills. Transport from residence to office or works is excellent, rarely requiring over fifteen minutes. The parts of the town in which the workers live are also pleasant and green; since the war a considerable number of housing estates have been built rather on English lines. Many of the workers live on the shores of the lake, and come to their work in Zurich on the national electric railway. A worker living seven miles from the city can get a monthly contract for six daily return journeys a week for seven shillings. In short, Zurich is beautiful, healthy, and convenient, in many ways a model town. But the City Council are far from satisfied. They intend to make the town much better than it is, and are prepared to spend money freely in planning out the best lines of improvement.

The Town Planning Department, which has no executive functions, but the whole of whose energies are devoted to the working out of plans, has a staff with salaries totalling £12,000 [1] a year, an astonishingly high figure when compared with any English city.

The city has from time immemorial had the power to purchase and own land; in fact at the present time it owns a quarter of its area, and another 3,000 acres, mainly of woods, outside its own area. Every year the City Council puts aside £25,000 for slum clearance. The city owns quite a substantial proportion of the slum area, and has a comprehensive plan for its rebuilding.

The City Council also takes an active interest in the cultural life of the city. There are in Zurich two universities, the famous Swiss Federal Institute of Technology which is financed by the state, and Zurich University, financed by the canton. The city itself contributes no less than £25,000 a year to the maintenance of the opera house; a guarantee of £2,500 a year towards the rent of the theatre; further sums of £7,000 and £8,000 to the encouragement of music and painting respectively. This makes a total of over £40,000 as a yearly contribution from the municipality towards different forms of art. Some ten years ago there was a referendum in the city as to the subsidy to be paid to the opera house. The whole of the political parties represented in the Council, of which there are, under proportional representation, seven or eight (with the exception of one small group), were in

---

[1] The wealthy local authorities of London spent £3,000 per annum on the Greater London Regional Planning Committee up to 1932, employing Sir Raymond Unwin who was doing admirable work with a small staff. In 1932 they decided they could no longer afford this expenditure and disbanded the organisation.

favour of the subsidy. The people also voted in its favour by a majority of nearly two to one.

Clearly there is a strong feeling, both among the rank and file of the people and among their leaders, that it is the responsibility of the city to encourage art and to be prepared to pay for it. No English industrial city makes any attempt to encourage its cultural life, even distantly approaching what is done by Zurich.

The city is governed through a council, elected by proportional representation for periods of four years, which is very similar to the councils in British cities. There are, however, two features of the city government which are totally different. The first is the referendum. In all communes which are too large to hold a general assembly of all the citizens, some form of representative council is elected. The individual citizen is kept as closely as possible in touch with the work through the referendum, which is universal, not only in the big communes, but also in every canton in the state. It is used with varying frequency in different parts of Switzerland, but it exists everywhere; it is unanimously approved. My own previous experience of the general vote of the citizens had only been in connection with that abomination, the English town's meeting. These meetings, in my experience, are attended by groups with some axe to grind, who go to give a partisan vote. There is not enough public spirit among the mass of the people to get even a reasonable attendance of those who go on account of their disinterested sense of responsibility for public affairs; and if after the town's meeting the usual postcard poll of the ratepayers is taken, probably 10 per cent. vote, and here again the decision is apt to be uninformed, biased by private interest and unsatisfactory in the extreme.

The position in Switzerland is totally different, for one simple reason: there are in Switzerland a sufficiently large number of citizens who take an intelligent interest in public affairs, and who have a sufficient sense of responsibility to vote whenever there is a referendum. The result is that the small interested vote which in English towns dominates the poll is in Switzerland swamped by the mass vote of intelligent and public-spirited citizens. Not only in Zurich, but wherever one went, one found the opinion

that the decisions of the people expressed through a referendum were often conservative, but that in the long run
the referenda tend to give sensible opinions in the public
interest.

It is interesting to note that one of the accusations
commonly brought against political life in Switzerland is
that the Swiss, having been largely a nation of peasants,
are excessively parsimonious. The fact that two-thirds of
the citizens of Zurich have enough pride in their city and
enough love of music to vote for the very large subsidy to
the opera house is evidence that this alleged parsimony is
far from being all-powerful.

The second interesting and from our point of view
important feature of the government of the city of Zurich
is the Executive Committee. The people not only elect
the Council of 125 members, but also directly elect the
nine members of the Executive Committee. This committee is in full charge of the administration of the city.
It prepares all the business for submission to the City
Council; it carries out all the decisions of the Council.

Its members are almost always taken from the councillors
who have become known to the people as good administrators. They are, therefore, elected as politicians, and when
elected they remain members of their respective parties but
proceed at once to devote practically the whole of their
time to administration. Each member of the Executive is
given a department to administer. They meet together
regularly under the chairmanship of the president of the
city to discuss and settle all major matters of administration,
and to agree on the advice to be tendered to the City
Council on matters of policy.

The Executive at the present time includes a majority of
Socialists. The president, Herr Klöti, a man of sixty, is a
Socialist. He was elected by the people as president ten
years ago and has been twice re-elected. Herr Klöti gets
a vote substantially larger than the Socialist vote; many
middle-class people support him. He has spent his life in
municipal administration. He is clearly a man of first-
class quality, of considerable powers of leadership, and a
whole-hearted lover of his city of which he is, of course,
exceedingly proud.

The Executive reports to the Council as a whole; if a

minority objects to the decision of the majority this must
normally be suppressed. But the rule is not so rigid as in
the case of the British Cabinet; it does occasionally, though
very rarely, happen that the minority is allowed to express
an opinion contrary to the decision of the majority.

The members of the Executive attend the Council meetings, take part in the discussions, but do not vote. Their
recommendations are, of course, normally accepted. On
the other hand, they are turned down occasionally either
by the Council or on a referendum, and so long as it does
not happen too often this does not in any way affect the
confidence with which the Executive are regarded.

It is the habit in Switzerland in most cases to continue to
re-elect members of the Executive so long as they are
willing to stand.

Having joined the Executive as politicians, the members
devote their energies to administration and are almost forced
to look at problems as administrators, and largely from
the point of view of the city as a whole, rather than of
their own department. They still continue to attend their
party meetings, which, as Herr Klöti told me, was most
important, because with their constructive outlook and
their administrative experience they are able to induce
their parties to avoid faction and to co-operate with other
parties in constructive work.

The members of the Executive at Zurich are paid about
£650 per annum, which would seem to be inadequate even
on Swiss standards, but it is generally agreed that so far
they have succeeded in getting men of high quality. Corruption is unknown.

The Executive appoint the administrative staff, including
the technical experts. They have authority to pay, and in
fact do pay, some of these technicians substantially higher
salaries than they receive themselves.

Although I was not in Zurich long enough to make any
sort of thorough study of the government, there can be no
doubt that it is on the whole efficient and imaginative.
The city owns and operates the ordinary trading undertakings: gas, electricity, trams, and water. Last year
it made a net profit of no less than £600,000 out of these
enterprises taken together, which is certainly evidence that
they are efficiently run.

As an example of Swiss social democracy, all burials are carried out by the city, which provides a hearse and one mourning carriage. These are invariably used by rich and poor alike, though if desired, of course, other carriages may be added. The provision of these by the city is free for all.

There is some feeling in Conservative circles that taxes have risen unduly in recent years, but feeling in this direction has not yet been strong enough to displace the Socialist majority, which is generally recognised as being moderate and businesslike.

BERN

Bern, with a population of 120,000, is the capital of Switzerland and of the Canton Bern, which has a population of 700,000. It is as beautifully situated, as clean, and as attractive a residential town as Zurich. It has the disadvantages which follow from being a smaller and rather poorer town, e.g., less attractive concerts, theatre, etc. On the other hand, it has the advantage that its beautiful woods and the surrounding country are easily accessible to the whole of the residents; for instance, the city has an open-air bathing-place on the banks of the river; when we visited it at lunch-time on a warm June day, there were actually over a thousand young men and women bathing and sun-bathing. This very attractive bathing-place is municipal; it is free to all, and very cheap meals are served; it also has the advantage that a large proportion of the youth of Bern can get to it in a few minutes from their places of work.

The government is run on similar lines to that of Zurich. I met several people actively concerned with it and as in Zurich was deeply impressed by their zeal, ability, and knowledge.

The Bern residents I met were unanimously of opinion that Bern is a better town to live in than Zurich. They are very proud of its history; it is a more beautiful town; it is more genuinely Swiss. When one suggests that it is too small, they retort that a generation ago, when the population was only 50,000, the cultural life of Bern was perhaps even better than it is to-day.

On the other hand, many people in Zurich regard Bern as

somewhat provincial, and a definitely inferior place to Zurich.

Several Swiss told me that not only is democracy in Switzerland based on the commune, but so also is culture; that most villages have their art, their singing, their drama. In Aarau, for instance, I found people most indignant if it was suggested that they were a satellite of Zurich. Aarau itself is the capital of the canton and is quite good enough for them.

Local tradition in Switzerland is immensely strong, and people generally are quite rightly very proud of their own town and canton.

THE CANTON

The canton is the traditional foundation of Swiss democracy. There are twenty-five cantons to-day, ranging from Nidwalden, with a population of 15,000, to Bern, with a population of 700,000.

The Swiss have a deep loyalty to their cantons; almost as much to those which are relatively young as to those which are 700 years old. Many hold that the liberty and independence of the Swiss citizen depend on the canton. Nothing is so much resented as centralisation—any attempt to increase the powers of the central government at Bern. One commonly hears that the canton is " the salvation of democracy "; that democracy lives and grows in the canton.

But most Swiss hold that, just as the canton is the basis of Swiss democracy, so the self-governing commune is the basis of cantonal democracy. There is no tendency whatever to aggrandise the canton at the cost of the commune. As we have shown, the communes have large powers of self-government. The business of the canton is to control and co-ordinate the communes, and to carry out such functions as they cannot deal with separately.

As we have said, there is the strongest objection to an increase of the powers of the state at the expense of the canton. In spite of this, circumstances have forced a steady movement in this direction for the last hundred years.

The state has for a long time dealt with foreign affairs,

the army, the post office, and the national railways. In recent years Switzerland has gone over to a protected economy; the state has been forced to undertake rapidly increasing duties in connection with tariffs, price control and industrial control generally, and social insurance. In 1850 the national budget was 4,000,000 francs; to-day it is over one hundred times as great.

The government of the cantons is of the usual Swiss type. A few of the smallest cantons are still governed by the famous Landesgemeinde, that is, a direct meeting of the whole of the people—when 10,000 people may assemble in the open air, with quaint old customs, to govern the canton; but in all other cases the government is by the election of a council and of an executive.

In the canton of Zurich the Executive of nine includes three Socialists, but curiously enough does not include any Roman Catholics, although about one-third of the residents belong to that faith. The middle-class majority in the Zurich cantonal Executive seems to work quite harmoniously with the Socialist majority in the Zurich municipal Executive.

The cantons, having very wide powers, naturally vary both in their constitutions and in their efficiency; some are very conservative, others more progressive. But it is surprising how universal are the forms and habits of democracy; how in every canton the political units are kept as small as possible; how the same devices are used for securing full responsibility of the individual, and the same device of the executive committee for securing democratic discussion.

I was told that one serious difficulty in Switzerland is that the taxes on property and income are in many cantons not adequately enforced. In some cantons the people assess their own incomes, and commonly assess them much too low. This causes acute difficulty when the state levies, as it does at present, a tax based on the cantonal estimates of property and income, some of which are correct, some of which may be grossly undervalued.

Another difficulty pointed out to me was that the cantons compete eagerly with one another to get factories and rich individuals into their canton. I was told by a competent authority that certain of the more unscupulous cantons have made offers of absurdly low taxation, inconsistent with their own laws, in order to attract rich men or companies.

But on the whole cantonal government seems to be honest and competent and certainly democratic.

There is undoubtedly a strong tendency for the state to get increased authority, the cantons therefore to lose it. But this does not seem strong enough at the present time seriously to threaten the important part the cantons still play in Swiss democracy.

THE STATE

The state is governed by the Federal Assembly, which consists of two separate and equal houses, the National Council of about 187 members, directly elected for four years by the whole of the people, and the Council of State, consisting of two members from each canton. Lord Bryce has called this the most businesslike legislative body in the world. There are about four sessions of three weeks each in the year; the houses meet at 8 o'clock in the morning. The chairs are arranged in semi-circular form, each member with a comfortable chair and desk; most of them spend their time reading the daily paper. Each member has a loudspeaker and an earphone. Those who want to listen to an inaudible speaker often sit or stand most informally near his desk. There is little oratory, and speeches are short; a division takes about a minute and a half inclusive of the time for members to come into the room, as against ten minutes in our House of Commons.

At present the membership of the National Council is divided among the parties as follows:—

	Per cent.
Socialist	28
Liberals	24
Catholics	20
Peasants	11
Young Peasants	3
Sundry	14

Elections are by proportional representation, and the votes of the parties are fairly constant, only varying by a relatively small amount from election to election. There is no Government and no Opposition in the English sense of the words; in many ways the discussions are more like those of one of our big city councils than those of our Parliament.

The Federal Executive has seven members. They deal with all the business for the two houses of parliament, advise on legislation, prepare bills, etc., and carry out all the administrative work.

The individual members are elected at a joint meeting of the two houses, not by proportional representation; so that a majority of the electing body can if it desires elect the whole of the members of the Executive. In fact, there is an understanding between the Liberals, the Conservatives, and the Peasants Party; the constitution of the present Executive is as follows :—

Name	Age	Party	Department
Meyer	68	Liberal	Finance
Motta	67	Conservative	Politics (Foreign)
Baumann	64	Liberal	Justice
Obrecht	56	Liberal	Industry & Agriculture
Minger	57	Peasants	Defence
Pilet	48	Liberal	Railways & Post Office
Etter	47	Conservative	Education & Health

The members are paid 28,000 francs per annum and are strictly prohibited from earning anything outside. They are granted a pension of 60 per cent. of this amount after ten years.

It is generally regarded as a great honour to be elected, and there is said to be no difficulty in getting good men. One of the present members gave up positions bringing him in about 100,000 francs a year in order to become a member of the Executive. An American observer said in 1931 that the members of the Federal Executive " continue to be grossly overworked and grossly underpaid; but not one of them has ever been guilty of corruption in office ". [1] One of the members is elected each year as President. He presides at the meetings of the Executive, retains responsibility for his department, and has certain ceremonial duties. In practice his influence is very little increased by his position as President, and one often finds that even the politically minded Swiss do not know the name of their President. I had an interview with the President, who

[1] *Civic Training in Switzerland*, Brooks, p. 6.

was informal, simple, and friendly.   He showed me the room in which the National Executive meets; he did not send for a porter, but with some trouble found the key and the electric lights himself.

Although it is generally agreed that the members of the Executive are of good quality, it is held by many that there is no man among them now of outstanding driving force. The habit of re-electing them is so strong that it is almost an invariable rule for a man, once elected, to stay on till retiring age.

The Socialists regard the present majority as a middle-party coalition against the workers. They have long demanded places in the Executive which have hitherto been refused, though they hope that at the next vacancy a Socialist may be elected.

A leading Socialist told me that he regarded the action of the Liberals in England in 1923, in putting the Labour Government into power, as indicating a tolerance and broad-mindedness of which, in his opinion, the middle-class parties of Switzerland would not be capable.

The Socialists point out that a large number of economic and financial laws have been passed by Parliament during the last few years on the advice of the Executive as " urgent". This means that these laws are not submitted to the re-ferendum.   They also argue that they got a very large vote on an important referendum in 1933 against the deflationary policy of the Government and that in fact they were within sight of victory on this occasion.   They hold that this frightened the middle-class parties, who have since used their majority in an unfair way to get through financial legislation which the Socialists believe might be rejected on a referendum.

While I was there an important finance bill was being discussed for the purpose of providing urgently needed funds for the expenditure to which the state is committed. It was a compromise bill between the views of the right, who want indirect taxation, and those of the left, who want increased personal taxes on income and capital, especially of the rich.   The bill, having passed the Council of State, was finally rejected by the National Council by one vote.   This bill was to have gone to a referendum; the whole position is now more confused than ever.   There is a strong feeling on the part of some people that the majority is using its power unfairly in financial matters, and of others that there is a definite lack of competent leadership. The financial position seems to be a very serious problem for Swiss national democracy.

There is strong feeling among the left against the use of the " urgency " method of avoiding referenda, and on the initiative of the Socialist Party a proposal defining and limiting the conditions under which the " urgency " method may be used will be submitted to the people in a few months' time.

While I was in Switzerland there was a good deal of discussion as to whether the cantons should each continue to have its own criminal law, or whether there should be a single criminal law for the whole state. The general view in German Switzerland was that so large a number of different codes of criminal law was absurd and dangerous, and that the only class which could be in favour of such an anomaly was the criminal class. The lawyers in French Switzerland shared this view. But many people in the French cantons were in the mood to resent anything that might be construed as dictation by the German majority, and were strongly opposed to the national criminal law for this reason. There was also some opposition to it on the ground that the powers of the cantons are being continually decreased, and that the handing over of the criminal code to the national Parliament would be another nail in the coffin of the cantons.

The referendum was held on July 3rd, 1938, and the introduction of the single national criminal law was carried by a small majority: 352,000 votes against 310,000.

The chief value of the referendum in national affairs is probably its effect in educating the people—in interesting them in great affairs as well as in small. National referenda have been comparatively rare recently.

On the whole there is less to be learnt from national political institutions than from those of the canton and commune. It seems probable that the two typical Swiss institutions, the referendum and the executive committee, are more effective in the canton and in the commune than in the state. In these days of wars and threats of wars, and of urgent financial and economic problems, it is doubtful whether the National Executive Committee provides sufficiently effective leadership and sufficiently rapid decision.

CONCLUSION

Lord Bryce wrote in 1921:[1] " The most interesting lesson Switzerland teaches is how tradition and institutions, taken together, may develop in the average man, to an extent never reached before, the qualities that make a good citizen—shrewdness, moderation, common sense, and a sense of duty to the community. It is because this has come to pass in Switzerland that democracy there is more truly democratic than in any other country."

The good fortune of the Swiss is that their history began among small groups of people living in secluded mountain valleys, who came together for common defence against foreign tyranny, and gradually built up the present communes and cantons and finally, based on these small and almost completely self-governing units, the national state. Swiss democracy has grown almost entirely from below, and even to-day the commune is generally regarded as the foundation, and the most essential part, of Swiss democracy.

Swiss history is thus based on geography, on the division of the country by mountains into a large number of partly isolated units. And Switzerland owes another debt to geography. There is no coal or iron; the only industrial asset is water-power, which provides cheap electricity. It is a remarkable tribute to the ability and industry of the people that in spite of this lack of natural resources they have built up an important export industry in engineering. But for these reasons their industry generally is in small units, and fits in admirably with the cantonal system.

Similarly, there are no great plains suitable for the large-scale growing of wheat; geography and climate conspire together to make the country suitable for small-scale peasant agriculture based on grass and cattle.

Natural conditions are thus responsible for the development of small political units, of small-scale agriculture and industry. They may fairly be regarded as the originating

[1] *Modern Democracies*, Vol. II, p. 449.

cause of Swiss democracy. But the Swiss people have taken the fullest advantage of the opportunities offered them. They have reinforced the effect of these natural conditions by inventing political machinery admirably adapted to preserve and strengthen their traditional democracy. Three Swiss institutions seem to have outstanding importance.

First, a series of devices which bring home political power and responsibility to every citizen: the small size and wide powers of the commune and of the canton, the close contact of every citizen with the whole of the problems of government, and with their political leaders, the immense amount of voluntary administrative work carried out in the communes by the ordinary citizen. Every Swiss is a member of a commune; it is only those who live in the few large towns who are not expected several times in the year to attend the political assembly of their commune—a magnificent piece of education for citizenship; and the relatively small number who live in the few large towns have not only the ordinary duty of electing a council and usually several other bodies, but also in every case the responsibility, through the referendum, for all major decisions of policy.

Secondly, we have in every Swiss political unit the device of the Swiss executive committee where three, five, seven, or nine leading members, almost always of different political parties, are elected to lead the government They are elected from among the leading politicians, they are given a whole-time administrative job, they are forced to agree among themselves on policy. In this way every question is, even in its early stages, discussed among the most qualified and experienced leaders of different parties. It is an excellent device for securing one of the essentials of democracy—the constant search for agreement by discussion and persuasion. These men become, to the extent of perhaps 90 per cent., administrators working for the general good, to the extent of perhaps 10 per cent. they remain party politicians. They attend party meetings and are, therefore, in a position to influence the parties away from faction and towards the habit of thinking constructively, and of putting the common good above party advantage.

As regards village or city government, it seems to me there can be hardly any doubt that this system is far superior to our British system; one can scarcely see in theory how, if it is properly worked, it can fail to give both more effective leadership and closer co-operation between the parties; and from what I have seen of Swiss cities I have little doubt that this is substantially true in practice.

As regards the national government, the position is somewhat different. The British cabinet system would seem likely to give more effective leadership than the Swiss executive system; and in fact there is at the present time a good deal of dissatisfaction with the lack of leadership in Swiss national affairs.

Thirdly, we have two great democratising forces in the schools and the military service system. With insignificant exceptions all go to the same schools on terms of absolute social equality. A hotel manager told me that he had recently attended the twentieth anniversary of his school-leaving year; among those present, all of whom addressed one another as " *du* ", were people of all classes: a railway porter, a tram driver, a municipal employee, a bank director. Those who had achieved wordly success were treated in exactly the same way as everybody else.

It is well known how powerfully the system of military service, universally compulsory on rich and poor, who are treated exactly alike, also reinforces the social sentiment of democratic equality.

There are, of course, difficulties and imperfections. Economic and class problems are the most intractable and the most likely to cause trouble. The solution of the religious difficulties seems almost complete, but some race feeling is still apt to crop up at times. The French-speaking area, with only half the population of the German-speaking area, is always ready to resent any appearance of majority dictation. On the other hand, the threat from the foreign dictatorships is a most effective cement. It has done much in the last two or three years to improve the relations between the Socialist Party and the trade unions on the one hand, and the capitalists on the other. No Swiss, whether speaking German or French or Italian, is willing for an instant to abandon the self-governing freedom of his commune and his canton to become an insignificant unit, governed from a distant centre by some unknown autocratic authority. This seems to apply almost as strongly to democratic but centralised France as it does to Germany and Italy.

On the whole there can be no doubt that Lord Bryce was right in his praise of the high democratic qualities of the Swiss. Perhaps the simplest test of educated citizenship is the kind of press which a country supports. In Switzerland there is an immense variety of small papers; no single paper with a circulation of 100,000, but 500 separate papers in total. On the whole the papers are full of serious matter; headlines are almost non-existent; few illustrations; very little sensation, crime, or divorce.

The Swiss are often accused of being dull. It is true that the *Neue Zurcher Zeitung* compared to the *Daily Blare* is dull for the uneducated. It is true that the Swiss love peace and freedom and do not indulge in war, nor in violent and dramatic party fights. What other country allows every citizen to keep his military rifle in his own home? and can be sure that its citizens are sufficiently " dull " not to use the rifles for revolutionary purposes!

Does anybody call his Swiss guide—usually an ordinary peasant—dull? Or rather friendly, intelligent, thoughtful, and utterly reliable? Can anybody call Zurich, perhaps the pleasantest town of Europe to live in, dull? Would that we had more of Zurich's " dullness " in Manchester!

The Swiss believe in education, and in the search for agreement and for wisdom through discussion and persuasion. The mass of the citizens are moderate, friendly, independent, and efficient; the leaders are honest, keen, competent, cultured, and surprisingly modest. I met a good many, from the President downwards, and was impressed by their knowledge of affairs, of history, and of the principles of democracy, by their keenness and capacity; but above all by their modesty. I never heard one of them talk about what " I " have done. It was always " we ". They were interested and absorbed in their job with a quite remarkable absence of vanity.

Finally, the Swiss have achieved the most difficult and essential task of democracy: they have an active and widespread public opinion, sufficiently informed and responsible to vote sensibly on all big questions, to resist the pressure of interested groups, and to over-rule them at the polls. Therefore, the referendum works well, and is so firmly established that its continuance is not questioned in a single commune or canton throughout the country.

As Lord Bryce puts it, one can rely on " the good sense and good temper " of the Swiss people as a whole. Democracy works perhaps best in a village like Blatten, where life is on a small scale, stable and simple. But it also works with astonishing and encouraging success in the larger towns, in the cantons and in the country as a whole. To quote Salvador de Madariaga :—

" In the midst of a Europe in which the conflicting characters and ambitions of Germans, French, and Italians are a constant source of irritation and war-mongery, Switzerland has become a haven of peace composed precisely of Germans, Frenchmen, and Italians who have decided to build up a Commonwealth across their differences, as if to show the world that it can be done and how.

" All these paradoxes have but one key. The Swiss have achieved all these apparent impossibilities because they have made up their minds to do so. *Switzerland is a creation of the human will.* Now, the human will differs from mere human impulses in that it is intelligent and purposeful. Knowing whither it goes, it studies the way. Knowing the way, it keeps to it.

" And since it is evident that the specific feature of Western civilisation is precisely that it seeks to achieve clear aims by the operation of the human will, it follows that Switzerland is the prototype of our Western civilisation and the masterpeice thereof."

CHAPTER III

SWEDEN

" From Sweden comes news of a rare fiscal miracle, an unprecedented boom ; and a new technique of outmanœuvring depressions. This smart and prosperous little country has discovered how to put through social reforms without troubling business confidence. Administered by Socialists, kind to capitalists, present-day Sweden is a lesson in New Dealism without tears—and almost without debts.

" Sometimes the inhabitants themselves complain that nothing happens in Sweden—the country is too happy. The headlines reflect neither imperial ambitions nor labour fratricide. In the last five years, for instance, nothing has happened, except that Sweden has created the greatest boom in her history, the greatest boom in any peaceful country to-day. Industrial production is 50 per cent. above the 1929 peak with mills, mines, forests, and factories producing at almost 100 per cent. capacity. Unemployment is reduced to a minimum and the national income can buy 25 per cent. more than ever before. The government has emerged from five years of extensive agricultural subsidies and public works with a healthy budget and a startling method of handling depressions. . . .

" The incredible fact to be noted by Americans of every stripe is that Sweden has gone in for a far reaching New Dealism without scaring, overtaxing, or otherwise discouraging private enterprise and investments. . . . Sweden's experiment is worth reporting, not only because Sweden is half the distance again ahead of the 1929 milestone at a time when the U.S. is still struggling to get back there, nor because Sweden is at the same time ready and waiting for the next depression, but because she has achieved those two miracles without the sacrifice of essential democracy."

This quotation, which is taken from the American magazine *Fortune* for September 1938, is typical of the kind of thing that is freely being said about Sweden to-day, especially in the United States. Perhaps most has been done by *Sweden : The Middle Way*, by Childs, to make people believe that great and exciting things are happening in Sweden. They have abolished unemployment—it has been done by a Socialist Government—everybody is happy! So I arrived in Sweden full of interest and hope. I try in the following chapters to set forth my conclusions as to how far these things are really taking place.

Natural Conditions

Conditions in Sweden are in many ways different from those in Switzerland. In the first place, Sweden has no minorities of any importance, either religious or racial; practically everybody belongs, at least formally, to the national church. Racial minorities are so tiny as to be negligible. Further, she is lucky in having enjoyed peace for 120 years; in having as her geographic neighbours, Norway, Finland, and Denmark, all small, democratic, and peaceful, and in lying outside the centres of European turmoil. She has no empire and her foreign policy is accordingly very simple.

Sweden is a large country, the area being double that of Great Britain, with a relatively small population of six millions. This small population is a great advantage in simplifying the problems of government. The heads of the government can be in personal touch with the leaders of different sections of the national life in a way which is impossible in England. It is true that the area of the country is large and communications not too good—to travel from Stockholm to some of the northern parts takes 36 hours; but all important people can be met in Stockholm from time to time. Political problems are of a much more manageable size. The tasks of the government do not compare in scale, pace, and complexity with those in Britain. The Prime Minister has plenty of time to think quietly over his problems; he has only a fraction of the responsibilities and the burdens of the British Prime Minister.

Turning to economic conditions, from the agricultural point of view the natural resources are fairly good; Sweden's chief wealth consists in her immense forests and her ample supplies of high-grade iron ore. World demand and prices have been good both for timber and iron products, and have contributed greatly to the successful export trade of the last few years. Another outstanding feature of Sweden's natural resources is, on the one hand, the complete absence of coal, and on the other hand, the many waterfalls, a source of cheap and ample power and heat.

Owing, no doubt, to the absence of coal, the development of industry in the modern sense was late, beginning only about 1870, and was from the early days based on hydro-electric power. The days of *laissez-faire* were already gone, and from the start the Swedes paid attention to planning for amenity as well as for profit. The foul works and slums of our early industrial age never developed in Sweden.

A further geographic advantage is that industry is decentralised. The location of the factories based on timber is settled by the forests and rivers, of those based on iron by the iron-ore mines. Deep-water rivers and lakes cover large areas of the country, making it possible for ships to come alongside works in the central areas.

An important advantage of the small size of the population is that economic inequality is much less than in large industrial countries. There are few very rich people, and there seem to be fewer very poor. Their economic problems are more easily manageable than ours, and the poverty of the slum areas of great cities is unknown in Sweden; one never sees rags or beggars.

HISTORY

In spite of the fact that until about thirty years ago the King nominated his own Cabinet of Conservatives and civil servants, there is a background of parliamentary government as far back as history goes. The "Things" had considerable independence of the King: the consent of the people, especially to new taxes, was at many periods

essential, and the rule of law in certain aspects has bound
King and nobles, as well as the people, from time
immemorial.

The people have had a good deal of responsibility for
local government over long periods; during the last
500 years local government has been of real independent
importance, not always, but for the greater part of the
time. Leading authorities hold that there is in Sweden
a long tradition of independent responsibility, especially
among the farmers and peasants, in strong contrast to the
history of Germany, and that this goes some way to account
for the success of democracy in Sweden as against its
failure in Germany.

Sweden is governed by a King, who is an hereditary
monarch, a Cabinet of twelve ministers, and the Riksdag
(Parliament), which is divided into two chambers, the
First (Upper) Chamber and the Second Chamber. The
First Chamber consists of 150 members elected by proportional representation for a period of eight years; the
Second Chamber is composed of 230 members elected by
the same method for a period of four years. Since 1809
there has occurred a gradual change in the distribution of
power, the Riksdag having steadily increased its influence
at the expense of the crown.

This movement has developed with remarkable rapidity
during the present century. The Conservatives held
undisputed power till about 1900. From that date the
Socialist and Liberal parties fought constantly and vigorously to increase the power of Parliament. In the earlier
days there was a syndicalist movement among the Socialists; they tended to rely mainly on industrial action to
improve the lot of the workers. There was a great strike
in 1909, called by some a general strike, fought by the
trade unions and supported by the Social Democratic party
under the leadership of Branting, the outstanding figure
in Swedish politics in the present century. It was completely defeated, and had a considerable effect in reducing
the belief in what it was possible for the trade unions to
achieve without the support of parliamentary action. The
defeat of the strike was the end of syndicalism in Sweden.
Since then the Social Democratic parliamentary party has
devoted its energy to parliamentary methods, under the

inspiration of Branting; though at the same time the strength of the trade-union movement has been steadily developed.

As a result of the combined efforts of the Socialists and the Liberals, democracy finally triumphed in 1920; a fully democratic constitution was adopted in that year. The elections are by proportional representation, direct election for the Second Chamber and indirect election by the members of the municipalities for the Upper Chamber. As a result of proportional representation in moderate-sized constituencies, there have emerged in Sweden four main political parties: the Conservative, Liberal, and Socialist, corresponding roughly to our parties, and a Country party, known as the Farmers party. There are also three or four other quite small parties which have not proved of any great importance.

The Socialist party grew steadily in strength, till in 1932, under the leadership of Per Albin Hansson (the present Prime Minister) and a very able group of men aged about forty-five to fifty, they formed the government which still continues in power, and so far as one can judge seems likely to do so.

From the moment of taking office they adopted a policy of social and economic reform, dealing with each matter on practical lines as it arose. They laid no stress on doctrinaire principles of nationalisation of industry. Their steady aim has been to secure a strong left-wing government, with the broad object of giving practical benefits to the poor in town and country alike. They call themselves Social Democrats; since they have formed the government they have consistently put democracy first and socialism second; that is to say, they have aimed at securing the kind of world which socialists desire by democratic methods, seeking agreement on all occasions by discussion and persuasion. On the other hand, nobody can accuse their democracy or their socialism of being timid. They have constantly combined moderation with effective action.

On taking office they immediately gave an interesting example of their attitude. Being a minority government, they had to get support either from the Liberal or the Farmers parties. It might have been thought that their natural supporters would have been the Liberals, with

whom they had worked for twenty years, but, as one of the
Socialist ministers has explained, the Swedish Liberal
party was, on the one hand, by no means a radical party;
for instance, its policy was not nearly as advanced as that
of the English Liberal party embodied in the English
Liberal Yellow Book, which advocated a line very similar
to that which the Swedish Socialists have in fact followed.
Then, again, the Liberal party was inevitably jealous of its
former allies, whose strength continually increased, whilst
itself, once the biggest party in Parliament, was losing votes
and seats.   There was also strong hostility among influential
Liberals against the expansionist financial policy of the
Socialists, which they considered unsound, wasteful, and
socialistic.

On the other hand, it was true that the Farmers were not
socially advanced; they were a party with one aim, to
obtain the best possible prices for agricultural products,
and, as the Socialist minister added, it is easy enough to
make a bargain with a party which simply wants financial
concessions.   As it happened, the world slump had reduced
prices to such a low level that the standard of living of the
peasants and agricultural workers was being forced down
to almost starvation point.   The Socialists took the broad
view that there ought to be a good standard of living both
for the industrial and for the agricultural workers, and that
it was their business as a government to hold a just balance
between the two.   It was advantageous to each of them
that the other should have good wages and good purchasing
power, which would be helpful both to industry and to
agriculture.

The agricultural products of Sweden are exported only
in small quantities (except timber products, which have
maintained a consistently good price), and since the country
has been prosperous it has been possible to guarantee prices
for agricultural products in the home market which have
been regarded by the farmers as reasonable.   At the same
time, the standard of living of the industrial workers has
been good and improving.   The great increases in direct
taxation which have been imposed by the Socialist Government fall most heavily on the rich and middle classes, less
heavily on the farmers and industrial workers, who on the
other hand are the classes which benefit most by the

increasing social services. Under these fortunate circumstances, the Government has succeeded in holding the balance between the peasants and workers in such a way as reasonably to satisfy both.

The Socialists carried on a minority government for four years with the support of the Farmers; after the elections in 1936 a definite coalition of Socialists and Farmers was formed, which is governing the country to-day.[1] The municipal elections of September 1938 were fought on national issues, because the composition of the municipalities determines the composition of the Upper House. The results were heavily in favour of the Socialists. The poll was larger than the general election of 1932, nearly up to that of 1936. The Socialists obtained 50·5 per cent. of the votes; for the first time they won an overall majority. It is commonly assumed that their vote will, if anything, continue to improve; this means that in two years the Socialists will have a majority in both houses of Parliament.

Economic Achievement

As a result partly of good luck, partly of the good management of its predecessors, the Socialist Government in 1932 found itself economically in a good position. Taxation

[1] The Socialist vote was substantially increased at the election of 1936, when the parties were returned to Parliament in the strength shown by the following table:—

Table I

	Lower House Seats in 1936.	Upper House Seats in 1936.
Government:		
Social Democrats .	112	66
Farmers party .	36	22
	148	88
Opposition:		
People's party (Liberals) .	27	16
Conservatives .	44	45
Left Socialists .	6	1
Communists .	5	—
	82	62
Totals .	230	150

was low; there was no foreign debt; there was no internal national debt.[1] On the contrary, there was a net profit each year from the national undertakings, such as railways, forests, etc., which made an annual contribution to the budget. The rate of real wages had increased at an astonishing pace. In 1930 it was three times as high as in 1870. While Sweden was a very poor country in 1870, Professor Ohlin estimates that the standard of living is now about equal to that in England.[2]

Under these conditions, it was easy for the Socialist Government from 1932 onwards gradually to raise taxation, as shown in the following table:—

Table II

Income Tax (per cent.)

	Income £100		Income £1,000		Income £50,000	
	1930	1939	1930	1939	1930	1939
Earned . .	4	5	12	16	27	40
Unearned . .	5	9	15	32	36	67

Roughly speaking, the Socialists have in about six years doubled the taxation on unearned income, and increased the tax on earned income by 25 per cent. on the poor, and by no less than 50 per cent. on the rich.

It is true that the rate of direct taxation on large incomes is not even now as high as in England, but there is double taxation in the sense that the income of companies is separately taxed; in any case the very rapid increase of taxation in times of peace is remarkable. What is still more remarkable is that there has been no really serious protest. There are, of course, taxpayers' associations, which exist for the sole purpose of fighting increases of taxation; it is true that the Conservative party has constantly protested and fought against increases. But, in fact, they have been accepted and have left no bitterness.

[1] The income from the state-owned assets to-day exceeds charges on the internal debt by about five million pounds each year.

[2] *The Annals of the American Academy of Political and Social Science*, May 1938, p. 2.

As a result of this increased taxation and improved economic conditions, the national income from taxes increased at an astonishing speed. The Finance Minister, Wigforss, shows that in the four years from 1934 to 1938 the national income from taxes on income and capital increased by 60 per cent.; the total tax yield by 50 per cent.[1] This was due, on the one hand, to the increased rate of taxation, and on the other hand, to increasing wealth: industrial production had risen by 1937 to a level 50 per cent. higher than the previous peak of 1929. And this remarkable increase in tax income was achieved, as already pointed out, without arousing any feelings among the tax-paying classes sufficiently strong to cause any flight of money from Sweden or in any other way to endanger the economic wellbeing of the state.

With this large amount of money available, favours could without difficulty be distributed to all sorts of people. In the first place, the farmers had to be placated. The Prime Minister has said that there was a fairly serious Nazi movement among the farmers in 1932, but that from the moment when the Government guaranteed them a price of Kr. 2·30 per kilo of butter, the Nazi movement disappeared!

The bulk of the money has been spent in improving social services: [2] health and education were well developed when the Socialists came into power in 1932; other social services were relatively backward: great progress has been made in old-age pensions, poor and unemployment relief, and in social insurance. Competent authorities estimate that the social services in Sweden are now equal to those in England, and in some ways undoubtedly better, particularly hospital and health services. For instance, the hospital system and the fight against disease in general is being organised on a large scale and practically on a basis of free service according to need.

To give one example, in Gothenburg, which is a town of about 260,000 inhabitants, there are no less than 100 doctors in the service of the municipality. Ninety-nine per cent. of the hospital patients are attended to by the

[1] *Annals*, May 1938, p. 35.
[2] During the last two or three years there has been substantial and increasing expenditure on rearmament.

municipal services. Over four-fifths of the births occur in the municipal gynæcological hospital, where the charge is less than one shilling a day. A week in hospital for a confinement costs about seven shillings and sixpence including everything—attendance, food, medicine, and, if necessary, operations.

The out-patients department in the municipal ear, throat, and nose hospital is an example of the high standard at which they are aiming. The waiting-room is light and airy, delightfully furnished, with comfortable chairs, mural paintings, illustrated papers. I was told that nobody ever had to wait more than half an hour; after the first interview future visits are always by appointment and there is hardly any waiting. There are wards with one bed; the largest wards have four beds. The inclusive charge is two shillings a day. But if a patient wants a room to himself, which apart from the privilege of being alone is no better than the larger rooms, the charge is put up to twenty shillings a day. The whole thing is very pleasant, efficient, and democratic; the one exception being that the patients in the expensive private rooms get the services of the head doctor, whereas those in the general wards have to be content with assistants.

The Director-General of the Medical Board of Sweden summarises the Swedish views on matters of public health as follows:—

" It may appear from the presentation that health care and the care of the sick are in Sweden in certain respects becoming quite satisfactory, and that in some fields the achievements may even occasion some pride; but it should also be apparent that we are not satisfied with conditions as they are. The Swedish people have begun to regard sickness and premature death as a shame and a reproach. Therefore plans are being made to utilise those important findings of preventive medicine which have not yet to any great extent been applied in practice, and this program is on the whole designed to be completed during from five to ten years. A lively effort is being made to show that a democratic state, with the co-operation of all classes of the population, can improve its conditions of life and its capacity to utilise its possibilities to the full without the handicap of illness and economic disability. This is being done in the belief that the basic condition for efficient labor and for happiness in one's own life is complete physical and mental health.

" I believe that it can be said that the Swedish people at present are, by and large, inspired by one guiding thought: no matter how living conditions, working conditions, geographic locations, milieu, and race may vary, a modern state must seek to achieve one thing—the assurance of complete health to each and every one of its citizens." [1]

The present Government, while not pressing the traditional Socialist aim of nationalisation of the means of production, is beginning to talk of an alternative form of socialism: " the socialisation of consumption "; the idea behind this phrase being that only by government control extended into many varied fields will it be possible to give the whole of the people the opportunity of consuming what they need for national fitness, using the word " consumption " in the broadest sense to include not only food and clothing and housing, but also health and education and the other social services. It is held by many that the socialisation of consumption is a practical ideal and the best possible way of ensuring that every citizen shall as a consumer receive everything he needs for full physical health and fitness.

At the same time, it must be realised that these ideals are still a long way off; in particular, Sweden is badly behindhand in the provision of good working-class houses to be let at rents within the means of the poorest section of the population.

THE STANDARD OF LIVING

One of the best tests of the success of a government is the standard of living which it is able to achieve for the various classes of the people. I have tried very hard to find a statistician who would give a comparison between standards of living in England and the various Scandinavian countries, but with very little success. All statisticians agree that in the present state of their science it is impossible to give

[1] *Annals*, May 1938, p. 119.

more than very general figures in this matter. The best one can do is to quote the opinions of scientifically minded economists, who have had specially good opportunities of observing conditions in the countries concerned.

Swedish standards were carefully investigated by a group of English observers under the direction of Mr. and Mrs. G. D. H. Cole in 1936. Mrs. Cole sums up as follows: " The figures showing the earnings of various classes in Sweden as compared with those of their opposite numbers in Great Britain support a general impression that whereas over the greater part of the population the standard of living does not vary greatly as between the two countries, Sweden lacks both of our extremes—the black, helpless poverty of the depressed areas and the staggering superfluity which is flaunted in London shops and coldly exposed in the returns of death duties. In other matters than that of income purely, the same effect can be noticed; in education and in public health, for example, Swedish provision does not seem to equal the best that Great Britain can do, while being incomparably better than the conditions which Great Britain still allows to survive." [1]

I may also quote Professor Ohlin, the eminent economist and member of Parliament: " These and other figures indicate that the standard of living in Sweden is now comparable to that of the richer European nations, although still lower than in the United States and some other countries. Investigations into the consumption of certain foodstuffs corroborate this view." [2]

The standard of living is helped by the small size of the families, which is due to the very low birth rate. The net reproduction rate for the country as a whole is about 80 per cent. In Stockholm the position is extraordinarily bad: half the families occupying separate dwellings in the city actually consist of one person only; the net reproduction rate for the city is variously estimated to be between thirty and fifty, which means that a generation hence the number of women between 16 and 45 years of age will be between one-third and one-half of what it is now. But they are beginning to take this problem seriously, under the leadership of Professor Myrdal. A royal commission

[1] *Democratic Sweden*—edited by M. Cole and C. Smith, p. 5.
[2] *Annals*, May 1938, p. 2.

has investigated the problem and made several interim recommendations for reducing the financial burden of the child on the parent; some of these have been accepted, others are still under consideration by the Riksdag. The failure to produce enough children to maintain the population in so fine a race threatens to be a tragedy; and the solution of this problem is likely to become (given peace) the greatest and most urgent task before the country.

As regards the question of the extent of culture among the people of Sweden, it was impossible for me to go into this matter in the short time I was in the country. The beauty of their cities is famed all over the world.[1] The other day I came across a striking piece of evidence showing how widely the love of beauty is spread among the people. The Chairman of the British Design in Industries Association, which has for many years done pioneering work in endeavouring to improve the artistic quality of the designs used in a wide field of industry, informed me that the number of people interested in their work was confined to a small artistic élite. They had never been able to get over 800 members in Britain, whereas the Swedish society had no less than 75,000 paying members.

THE FORTY-HOUR WEEK

The Government has not allowed itself to be carried away by its rapidly increasing wealth; in everything it has shown typical Swedish moderation. An outstanding instance is the question of the forty-hour week, where the action of the Swedes is in vivid contrast with that of the Front Populaire in France. Blum, on doctrinaire principles, promised to reduce working hours from about forty-eight to forty, and at the same time to increase real wages. He seems to have convinced himself by " logical arguments " about the reduction of overheads that this was possible.

The Swedish Socialists fought for the forty-eight-hour week about 1920 and won it against prophecies of disaster. The Minister of Finance has pointed out that in three years the standard of living was higher than before. But they take the view that a further reduction in hours would

[1] See page 89.

not result in a corresponding increase in the rate of productivity, and that it would seriously reduce the volume of output and the capacity of the industries to pay high wages. The workers must, therefore, choose between a higher standard of living and increased leisure. So far they have worked for the higher standard of living, while endeavouring gradually to make the forty-eight-hour week really effective. As in all other countries, the forty-eight-hour week is not universally effective, especially in agriculture, and the Government is endeavouring to ensure that all classes are adequately protected by the forty-eight-hour week before taking further strong action to help the favoured sections. Meantime, however, they are making substantial improvements; legislation was passed last year providing for a fortnight's holiday with pay for practically all workers.

Sweden, though going through much more prosperous times than France, and with a much stronger left-wing government, has proceeded with northern caution, experimentally, step by step. She is fortunate in having some eminent and sensible economists, and perhaps still more fortunate in having a government which, unlike other governments, is inclined to listen to them.

UNEMPLOYMENT [1]

Another important piece of good management is in connection with unemployment. The Finance Minister is himself a highly competent economist, and has courageously adopted modern financial methods for dealing with unemployment. The Government has acted along three main lines. Firstly, the currency has been well managed; it was linked with sterling at the right time, and it has been possible to keep both the internal price level and the foreign exchanges steady. Secondly, the budget was deliberately unbalanced in the slump, and what is much more important and unusual, the deficit has been paid off in the recent boom years. Thirdly, public works policy was inaugurated rather late in the slump and was perhaps cut down rather late in the boom, but large quantities

[1] See Chapter IV.

of reserve work are now being prepared against the next slump, not only by the Government, but by the cities. Stockholm, for instance, will have a reserve of a million pounds in a few months' time waiting to be spent when required.

It seems to be generally agreed by economists that in all three branches the Government has acted correctly and with courage. Its action was undoubtedly of real assistance in getting out of the slump more quickly; and in reaching the position which has prevailed during the last two or three years, in which it can almost be said there is no unemployment—that is to say, there is only unemployment of what is called a frictional character, caused mainly by the delay in changing from one job to another. It is perhaps fair to characterise in the language of ordinary daily intercourse the position in Sweden during the last two or three years as being one of no unemployment. Perhaps an even more remarkable achievement is the fact that they have managed to avoid the vicious spiral of rising wages and prices, which normally accompany boom conditions, nor is there any undue boom on the stock exchange.

TRADE UNIONS

But Swedish powers of co-operation are by no means confined to the Government. The relations between capital and labour are also good. Collective bargaining is almost universally recognised; both employers and trade unions have been organised in single powerful national federations since about 1900.[1] Both federations have large reserves of money. Relations between the two have on the whole steadily improved since the great strike of 1909. By consent of both sides, the unions have become more and more industrial, that is to say, a single union covers all the workers in an industry; so that demarcation disputes are rare. Piece work is general and is widely supported by the trade unions, owing to the sensible co-operation of the employers in avoiding the usual troubles of piece work when

[1] It is said that industrial labour in Sweden is more fully trade-unionised than in any other country; they have a membership of nearly 900,000.

C

incompetently administered, due to the constant and unfair cutting of rates. The universal habit of collective bargaining, the prevalence of piece work, and the avoidance of demarcation disputes, must be an important factor in avoiding certain glaring inefficiencies which exist in some sections of British industry.

A further proof of the moderation and good sense of both sides is that when a large number of agreements had to be renewed in the boom time of 1937, this was done without serious difficulty; there was only one very small strike.

The trade unions furnish most of the sinews of war to the Social Democratic party. This gives the unions considerable political influence; and on the other hand, prominent trade unionists who are closely associated with the responsible leaders of the nation can more easily understand that there is a national point of view, which, even when it comes into conflict with their own immediate interests, is worthy of consideration. This is a factor which makes for peace in the labour market.

POLITICS

Turning to the political side, I have already shown that the Government has held the balance between worker and peasant during the last six years so successfully as to secure increasing support from both. I have also shown that it has managed its economic affairs well and has not too seriously antagonised the capitalist classes.

It is, of course, not possible to describe in an essay the measures by which the Government has achieved these remarkable results. Broadly, its actions have been marked by good sense, good temper, and moderation. On the whole, party seems to count for less than in England, and the effort at sensible constructive legislation for more. For instance, obstruction in Parliament is unknown, and it is said that any attempt at obstruction would be regarded with general disapproval and contempt.

SOCIALISATION

Broadly speaking, the policy of the Socialist Government has been not to fight or to interfere with capitalist production, but to give it every opportunity for efficient working; to tax it for social services, and to control it in the public interest where necessary. The Government owns the railways, a large proportion of the water power, and has a large interest in the iron-ore deposits. But it is typical of Sweden that almost the whole of this nationalisation was carried through in pre-Socialist days by Liberal or Conservative governments! The Socialists have merely added to the existing nationalised assets with their usual moderation.

The manufacture and sale of drink were also nationalised by middle-class governments (because of excessive drunkenness), and a government monopoly of tobacco introduced. The Socialist Government has suggested monopolies of petrol and coffee for revenue purposes, but has not been able to carry them through.

CO-OPERATION

The growth of the co-operative movement in Sweden is an important example of the power of the Swedish citizens to work together in their common interest. The consumers' co-operatives are well developed and are united in a national Co-operative Union, which has become a powerful element in the economic life of the country. Its assets amount to eleven million pounds, and it has 4,400 retail shops and a total membership of more than 600,000.

The main object of the Union is to protect the interests of its consumer members by keeping price levels of consumers' goods as stable as possible, and it has in several instances succeeded in breaking up trusts and in keeping down prices: the classic case being its achievement in breaking the international ring in electric lighting bulbs and in reducing the price by something approaching 50 per cent. With this aim in view, the Union has also taken up the manufacture of various goods, much on the lines of our own Co-operative Wholesale Society, and its annual output in this field has recently been officially stated to be seven million pounds. Among its industrial activities are margarine factories, oil refineries, coffee-roasting plants, factories for rubber goods, flour mills, a staple fibre factory, a cattle-food cake factory, etc. Although the bulk of the output is for home consumption, some products have lately found a market abroad. By this means the Union brings constant pressure to bear on combines manufacturing consumers' goods in large quantities, so that they are forced to adapt their price policy to that of the Union.

There is no doubt that the Swedish Co-operative Union is remarkably successful, but exaggerated claims are sometimes made for it. As a matter of fact, the whole of its range of manufacture does not produce more than about 2 per cent. of the total national production of industrial goods.

An important development of the last ten years has been the rapid growth of producers' co-operation in agriculture. A leading agriculturalist writes: "Agricultural co-operatives handle somewhat more than 60 per cent. of the principal agricultural products. . . . To those who at close range have studied the development of agricultural co-operation in Sweden, it is clear that it has had an extra-ordinary importance for agriculture as an occupation and for farmers as an occupational group. For agriculture it has created more dependable outlets, more orderly assembling and processing, and has made possible a note-worthy improvement in quality production. In the last analysis, the results of all this redound to the public good. For the farmers it has been, by reason of its democratic character, a real education in economic problems, and they have gained knowledge even as to how agricultural pro-duction itself should be planned. Its significance for the immediate future in all these respects may be even greater, provided its endeavours continue to be directed to the same ends as at present." [1]

While there is no doubt of the economic advantage of co-operation in Sweden in the provision of cheap goods for the mass of the people, there is a good deal of idealism behind it. A Swedish authority has said: " Their strength

[1] *Annals*, May 1938, p. 199.

and importance depend quite as much on ideology as on
purely material conditions. Members of agricultural
co-operatives think of the glory of working the earth and
of maintaining the dignity of the farmer's profession.
Members of consumers' co-operatives think of the time
when their system, instead of capitalism or state socialism,
will govern the economic relations of mankind."

CIVIL SERVICE

One interesting point is the difference between their
civil service and ours. Civil servants in Sweden have
from old times enjoyed very high social prestige; it is said
that forty years ago a junior clerk in the Treasury was
much more highly regarded in society than a big business
man. They are generally competent, and although the
pay is relatively low, corruption is almost non-existent in
the national civil service, though it is said to occur to some
extent in local government. There are hardly any salaries
substantially exceeding £1,000 per annum. The high
civil servants are given a good deal more independence
than in England. In the first place, they are allowed to
be members of parliament, and there are at present actually
a good many civil servants in the Riksdag.

It is interesting to learn that in spite of the conservative
tradition of the civil service, the Socialist ministers report
that (in contrast to the democratic governments in
Germany) they have received willing service and un-
stinted co-operation from the whole of the civil service.
The success of those of the civil servants who go actively
into politics in keeping separate their duties as politician
and civil servant is illustrated by the fact that the Socialists
have appointed thirteen provincial governors during their
period of office, and that only six of these are Socialists.

In the second place, several government departments
include one or more " boards ". These boards consist of
senior civil servants; they are separate legal entities with
definite powers and a considerable degree of independent
authority. For instance, the Ministry of Social Affairs
has a medical board with a senior civil servant at its head.
These boards deal on their own responsibility with all

routine administration within a clearly defined field, and, of course, they give advice to their minister, and through him to the Government and to the Riksdag, usually in the form of reports. It is, in general, the duty of the board to make reports on all important matters which come before it.

The interesting thing is that not only are these reports themselves available to the public, but the general correspondence and decisions of the board are equally open; in fact, the whole administration is available for the information of the public. There are inevitably many exceptions to this, especially in foreign affairs, but this is the general rule. This means that any matter of public interest is likely to be discussed in the press before it is discussed in Parliament, and in contradistinction to what happens in England, the whole of the information available to the Government is also available to the public and to the individual members of Parliament. This habit of trusting the public with full information on which government decisions are based is an example of the Swedish democratic spirit, of their confidence that information will not be abused, but will, on the contrary, be likely to lead to a wiser public opinion. It often involves a public difference of opinion between the minister and his leading civil servant advisers, which we in this country would consider an awkward situation, but nobody in Sweden seems to see any objection to this.

The system is so different from ours that it is difficult to bring out its essential features in a few pages. It is a subject which would well repay study in England. Meantime the following comment on the above summary from a leading Swedish statesman is of considerable interest :—

" I suppose the boards might best be described as a kind of ' permanent commission ' making researches and giving independent opinions before decisions are taken by the Government. It gives a false impression to say that the Riksdag has to decide when there are differences of opinion. Government — or officially ' Kingly Majesty ' or shorter ' the King '—and Parliament are the only powers. The boards belong to the earlier phase, when the questions are under consideration, before the Government have taken a decison to introduce a bill. The boards are also consulted with regard to questions that don't go to Parliament, but are decided by the Government alone. But it is a very important fact that in this way controversial questions often come up for public discussion at an early date. The civil servants of the ' boards ' are not considered ' servants of a minister '. The ministries or departments have their own civil servants, who prepare the decisions of the Government."

While it is surprising to us that the high civil servants should be semi-political and semi-independent of their ministers, it is a system that works well in Sweden; its success is striking evidence of the strength of the democratic tradition of civic responsibility.

No Extremes

One of the best tests of a successful democracy is the strength or weakness of extreme parties believing in methods of violence. There have been, and still are, both Nazi and Communist movements in Sweden. The Nazis have never succeeded, even with the help of proportional representation, in electing a member to either house of Parliament. They are to-day weaker than ever. The Communists have at present six members in the two houses; they were fairly strong and extreme after the war; now they are generally held to be weaker than ever before and also more moderate. Considering that a moderate Socialist Government has been in power for six years, which, though it has greatly improved the social services, has socialised practically nothing, the fact that the left-wing extremists are to-day weaker than they were in 1932 is eloquent testimony to the success of the Government and to the moderation and good sense of Swedish democracy.

Education for Citizenship

In these days it is becoming more and more recognised that democracy must be not only moderate and tolerant but also efficient. Perhaps the most important task before the democracies is to show that democracy is consistent with effective leadership. Sweden is remarkable for the quality of her leadership. From the King downwards, the leaders in politics, in industry, and in social affairs are broadly characterised by moderation and efficiency. The Swedes are not easily susceptible to emotional oratory; it is a striking fact that no outstanding leader has appeared in the last twenty years either among the Nazis or the Communists, and that in spite of the moderation of the Socialist Government the left-wing movement to-day is generally considered to be weaker than it has been for a generation. The most important leaders to-day are, of course, the Socialist members of the Government, pupils of Sweden's outstanding political personality, Branting, former university student of astronomy. After a youth of agitation, Branting settled down as a constructive Socialist statesman, who carried weight not only in Sweden but in European politics. The group who now dominate the Cabinet in Sweden grew up under his influence, and it is fortunate for Sweden that they are men of extraordinary constructive ability, marked by the usual Swedish moderation, good sense, and good fellowship.

The Swedish educational system has some responsibility for Swedish leadership. Universal compulsory free education has been in force since 1834. The system is more democratic than ours in that they have nothing like our public schools, though there are a small number of secondary schools for the sons of the rich. It is just as true in Sweden as here that a rich man can always get a secondary education for his son if he is ready to pay for it, while only a limited number of the children of the poor can get a secondary education as a result of passing a competitive examination. It is, however, true that a very large proportion of those in important positions in all walks of life in Sweden have, in fact, risen from quite poor circumstances.

It is interesting to note that the authorities lay considerable stress on the importance of teaching the children to understand the affairs of the modern world. The Riksdag has actually passed resolutions urging that history should be taught more on social lines and more in relation to the affairs of to-day; the title of the courses has been officially changed from " History " to " History and Civics ".

After leaving the elementary school, continuation classes
are compulsory to the extent of 180 hours a year for two
years. Civics is one of the three compulsory subjects in
these continuation classes.

Adult education on the lines largely of our Workers'
Educational Association, but with more local discussion
groups, has played an important part in the education of
Socialist leaders. The present members of the Cabinet,
though many of them came from humble circumstances,
are mostly very highly educated.

Striking evidence of the degree of civic education is
offered by the fact that Professor and Mrs. Myrdal's solid
400-page book on population, published a few years ago,
sold 15,000 copies. Allowing for the larger population,
this would be the equivalent of a sale of over 100,000 copies
in England.

One point on which Sweden differs markedly from
England is that professors in the social sciences are not
only listened to by the Riksdag but often are actually
members. There are at present eight professors of law in
the University of Upsala; five of them are members of
Parliament. The University of Stockholm has a strong
Faculty of Economics, of which the recent head was
Professor Cassel. His four leading pupils now hold the
following positions: Professor Myrdal, Socialist M.P.,
Professor Bagge, M.P., leader of the Conservative party,
Professor Ohlin, M.P., President of the Young Liberals,
and Professor Wohlin, M.P., Farmers party, head of
Customs. It is a remarkable coincidence that these four
economists, all pupils of one very distinguished professor,
should hold leading positions, one in each of the four
political parties! Clearly, even in Sweden, a thorough
study of economics by no means always leads to the same
conclusions on matters of practical politics!

The fact that so many of the leading professors in the
social sciences take an active interest in public affairs must
be a real benefit to the level of public discussion and of
legislation in Sweden, and must be very effective in avoiding
the danger of a purely aloof and academic attitude on the
part of the universities.

CONCLUSION

What is the future of Swedish democracy likely to be? Instead of expressing any personal opinions at this stage it seems best to try to summarise the views of responsible leaders of the Conservative and Social Democratic parties.

A Conservative View

An able and experienced Conservative leader expressed the following views as to the Social Democratic party. In the first place, he gave the usual arguments about Sweden's good fortune: she has had a hundred years of peace and security, with no racial or religious quarrels; she is detached from the turmoil of European politics; as a result of her magnificent supplies of timber and iron and the good prices which their products have commanded, the people have enjoyed a steady, rapid, and general increase in the standard of living and of security.

Sweden's economic success is due to the enterprise and high degree of technical ability of her people. Many important inventions have been made by Swedes and have become the basis of specialised branches of industry in high quality goods, such as ball bearings and telephones, which are exported against the competition of the whole world at good prices. In short, Sweden's highly technical, successful, and remunerative export trade is due to the initiative, energy, and ability of her inventors, scientists, entrepreneurs, and capitalists.

But quite apart from this the Socialist Government has been immensely lucky in that economic conditions have improved steadily ever since 1932 when it came into power. Taxes were at a fairly low level; even to-day, in spite of the great increases made by the Socialists, they are still lower than in England. Efficient industrial and agricultural production have provided constantly growing sources of income; the industrialists are making adequate profits and are contented. But it is essential to emphasise again and again that this great economic success is not due to democracy nor to Socialism; the only credit which the Socialists can claim is that they have not hindered it.

The Socialists have made many promises of higher

wages, increasing social services, better prices for agricultural products, and so on. By such promises they have been able to indulge in the mass purchase of votes, with which we Conservatives cannot possibly compete, and owing to sheer good luck they have been able to keep most of their promises. What is worse, the chief plank in our election programme was rearmament; owing to the threat of war, the Socialists are now rearming on a basis agreed with us: they have stolen our programme.

It cannot be denied that the Government is honest, competent, and moderate, and that it has the confidence of large sections of public opinion. As a result of all this, the Socialists are steadily gaining votes and are almost sure to continue to do so so long as times are good; almost inevitably they will shortly have a majority in both houses. Social democracy is a religion to them and their supporters: they are like the Catholic Church. It has been their systematic and deliberate policy to give all posts of importance to pliant party men; to reward party service and to destroy independence. Party discipline is exceedingly strict, the feeling of solidarity very strong.

Although things have gone well hitherto there are serious dangers ahead. It is widely feared in industrial circles that a development of the present trends may result in something like a Socialist dictatorship, and the undermining of the Swedish tradition of independence; from this point of view England is a sounder democracy than Sweden. The Socialists have already made attempts at dangerous proposals, such as state monopolies of petrol and coffee, and confiscatory death duties, which would destroy Sweden's capital resources. When the slump comes, as it inevitably must, they will no longer be able to keep their promises and will be forced to drastic action, either along lines of inflation or socialisation or the creation of new state monopolies which must lead to serious injustice and in the long run to national disaster.

A Socialist View

The following is an attempt to sum up the views of the Socialist leaders.

It is true, as the Conservative states, that Sweden has been lucky in her natural conditions. It is true further that the Socialist Government has been lucky in that conditions have been in some ways especially good since it came into power; in particular it has been possible to export timber and iron products at good prices.

It is true also that Swedish industry, both as regards the workers, inventors, technicians, and the managers, is competent, energetic, and successful; it is partly due to the help and guidance of the Government that employers and workers get on well together.

We have during our six years of government steadily pursued three main lines of policy. Firstly, to encourage industrial and agricultural production, at the same time controlling it, so as to prevent monopoly and exploitation and to ensure the lowest prices and the best possible conditions for the workers. Secondly, we have raised taxes in various directions; we have steadily improved the social services to such an extent that we venture to say that although there is, of course, still very much to do, we have almost revolutionised them in the last six years. Thirdly, we have pursued a policy of finance and public works which has not only enabled us to provide work for all (except for a small inevitable amount of frictional unemployment) but has also enabled us to avoid the dangers of boom conditions.

There are, of course, weak spots. There is serious poverty in some of the country districts. The flats in Stockholm are deplorably small, and overcrowding is bad for the large poor families. But on the whole Swedish democracy under our leadership is certainly a success; politically, economically, and socially, it provides the conditions to enable the great mass of its citizens to lead worth-while lives.

As a result of our good management we have gained the increasing confidence of the people; our vote has steadily increased, we now have an actual majority in the country and hope within two years to have a majority in both houses of Parliament. We have enthusiastic support from the whole left; so satisfied are the people that there is no party on the extreme left which is of substantial importance. On the other hand, we claim that the right, although they naturally abuse us, respect us, recognise that we are working in what we consider the public interest, and do not feel that we are treating them unfairly. There is no extreme party on the right advocating violence.

During the past six years we have done little in the way of socialisation, as other reforms have been more urgent. We have no immediate proposals for socialisation. Our policy has always been to consider the actual situation and to legislate step by step to improve conditions and standards of living. We intend to continue this policy. We cannot forecast to what extent and under what conditions socialisation may begin to be necessary; much will depend on the actions of the capitalists.

We recognise that if world conditions arise under which we cannot sell our exports, we shall be faced with serious difficulties. We are making every possible preparation to meet them, and feel that Sweden can meet such troubles as well as any other country, and that for Sweden our party can certainly meet them more effectively than any alternative government. Apart from any world cataclysm we are confident that we shall be able to continue our policy of dealing with the most urgent problems step by step, until ultimately we achieve a prosperous and just social order, such as the world has not seen before.

CHAPTER IV

HAS SWEDEN ABOLISHED
UNEMPLOYMENT?

PERHAPS the greatest weakness of the democracies in comparison with the dictatorships is their failure to deal with unemployment: two million unemployed in England, ten million in America. Many people think that the democracies can hardly survive unless they can eradicate this evil. The fact that Sweden is generally thought to have succeeded in abolishing unemployment is the main cause of the very wide interest in her achievement. For instance, so high an authority as Mr. Hugh Dalton allows himself to be carried away to the extent of writing as follows: " This book is a record and an explanation of what must seem, to dwellers in less happy lands, an economic miracle. In these last years Swedish Recovery, from trade depression and mass unemployment, has been sensational. External factors, such as the rise in certain export prices, have helped a little. But primarily the Recovery is due to internal action, based largely on the theories of Professor Myrdal, and executed with great political skill and economic insight by Ernst Wigforss, the brilliant Finance Minister in the Swedish Socialist Government." [1]

The leaders in the unemployment policy pursued by the present Swedish Socialist Government are two: Mr. Wigforss, Minister of Finance, and Mr. Möller, Minister of Social Affairs.[2]

They have written valuable articles explaining what has happened and what the principles behind it have been:

[1] *Monetary Policy and Crises*, by Brinley Thomas. Preface, p. x.
[2] A Swedish Liberal economist writes: " I think it less than justice to the Swedish unemployment policy of the period 1920–32 not to mention its main principles. Möller had to continue this policy in important respects."

in particular, the articles in the issue of the *Annals of the American Academy of Political and Social Science* for May 1938, which is devoted to an excellent series of essays on social problems and policies in Sweden, commemorating the tercentenary anniversary of the first settlement of Swedes in America.

In the first place, let us consider shortly the available statistics as to how far unemployment has, in fact, been abolished. The figures for the people who are seeking aid are given by Mr. Möller in the following table.[1]

Number of Unemployed.

| Year | Maximum Number | | Minimum Number | |
	Month	Number	Month	Number
1930	December	31,901	July	5,824
1931	December	88,761	July	30,520
1932	December	161,156	July	94,687
1933	March	186,561	July	138,855
1934	January	171,065	September	78,918
1935	January	93,419	September	41,190
1936	January	61,400	August	20,783
1937	January	33,509	August	9,577

These figures show a typical trade cycle, passing from the peak of one boom to the peak of another in a period of seven years. The minimum figure of unemployment at the peak of the two booms is remarkably low, but Mr. Möller points out that even in Sweden unemployment statistics are far from perfect. He estimates that the total number of unemployed at the bottom of the depression would be about 250,000, while the lowest figure of just under 10,000 given for August 1937 would, in his view, represent a total unemployment for the whole country of about 35,000. This is, of course, a very low figure. To show how high are the standards of the Swedish Government, Mr. Möller points out that Sweden has still two depressed areas to be dealt with; but he goes on to show

[1] *The Annals*, May 1938, p. 51.

that in one unemployment has fallen from 9,600 in December 1933 to 2,200 in December 1937, and in the other from 16,300 to 2,700 during the same period. Would that we could show equally successful achievements in our own depressed areas!

The table shows that there is a big increase of unemployment each year between the minimum, which occurs in the late summer, and the maximum, which occurs in the winter. This is due to the severe climate especially in the north of Sweden, which makes various kinds of open-air work impossible during the winter. It is very difficult to foresee any complete solution of this form of seasonal unemployment.

Mr. Möller states that in 1937 Sweden experienced the greatest boom which its economic history had perhaps ever known: the fact that the number of registered unemployed was a little higher than in 1930 was due to special circumstances—partly to the more liberal public assistance policy, which encouraged a higher frequency of registration.

One important success is that during the boom of 1937 and 1938 it has been possible to avoid the evils of boom conditions: the vicious spiral of rising wages and prices, the constant strikes in the readjusting of wages. Wage readjustments were made on a considerable scale almost entirely by friendly negotiations between the highly organised trade unions and the equally highly organised employers. Commodity prices rose quite moderately; nor was there any undue inflation of prices on the stock exchange. In fact, for the last two years Sweden has had the advantages of boom conditions, prosperity and full employment, and has avoided the disadvantages of unduly rising prices.

A COUNTER CYCLE POLICY

As Möller points out, what he calls their " general anti-crisis policy " has many different aspects.

" This anti-crisis policy consisted of a whole series of measures of a political–economic nature, co-ordinated, supporting each other, and of such a nature that independently, but especially jointly, they served the same end, namely, to create favorable conditions for a general economic revival and a victory over the crisis. A basic principle of the expansionistic policy which was formulated in 1933 was a planned co-ordination between the measures in the various fields of economic and social policy.

" In this series of measures one may include, in addition to the emergency projects, an agricultural policy which maintained the purchasing power of the farmers without increasing too much the living costs of other population groups; a financial policy which by financing public works through loans mobilized latent financial resources without too great a burden on the taxpayers; a monetary policy which aimed at a certain reflation of the price levels, of raw materials and industrial products while keeping the purchasing power of the consumer's krona as nearly constant as possible; and a foreign-exchange policy which smoothed the road for increased exports and made it possible to preserve relative freedom in trade with other countries." [1]

It is, of course, true that all these different lines of policy were pursued by the Government, but the basic idea underlying them was relatively simple. It is sometimes called " compensation ": at times of slump, when industry is depressed and has less money to spend and unemployment occurs, the Government steps in to maintain spending power; and at times of boom does what it can to reduce spending power, with the object of preserving a stable level of employment. Under the capitalist system, the determining factor as to the amount of employment is the number of persons who can be employed at a profit. For reasons not fully understood there is always a trade cycle covering a period of about seven to ten years: at a certain stage trade improves, profits are good, employment, prices and wages rise to boom conditions. Then gradually men lose confidence, and there is a steady decline down to conditions of slump. The effect of this is typically shown by the figures for Swedish unemployment on p. 79.

[1] *The Annals*, May 1938, p. 63.

In the past governments have acted just like private employers: in times of boom and prosperity they have spent freely; in times of depression they have economised. In this way they have added to the severity of the slump and to the height of the boom.

The policy now adopted by the Socialist Government in Sweden is sometimes called a " counter cycle policy ", under which the Government uses its powers to counter these cyclical tendencies of boom and slump. A private trader cannot do it; he must inevitably be guided by profit. If he employs less men in time of boom, he is deliberately throwing away profit; if he tries to employ more men in time of slump, he is likely to be ruined. The Government, on the other hand, is not subject to these influences and can, if it wishes, determine its expenditure, not on grounds of profit making, but on grounds of stable national employment. This policy has, of course, been advocated by economists, such as Sidney Webb and Keynes, for many years; but the Swedish Socialists are perhaps the first government to have made a serious attempt to put this principle into practice.

Prior to 1932 it had been " a cardinal principle of Swedish financial orthodoxy that the State should raise money by loan only for such purposes as would provide a return on the money expended. Other expenditure had to be met out of revenue, as had been the case with all the relief works up to this time.[1] And in 1932 Sweden was hardly in a condition to raise by taxation enough money to finance an effective programme of public works." [2]

The Socialists accordingly in fighting the election of 1932 threw financial orthodoxy to the winds, and demanded that the money necessary for a great programme of public works should be provided out of loans; they urged an immediate expansionist policy with free borrowing and unbalanced budgets. They did well in the election and formed a government with the support of the Farmers to pursue such a policy. They borrowed boldly,[3] they

[1] *Swedish Liberal Economist :* " Such was the theory: but there was a huge budget deficit in 1931–32."

[2] *Democratic Sweden*, p. 83.

[3] Comment by *Swedish Liberal Economist :* " The borrowing was not greater in 1933 and 1934 than in 1932."

openly unbalanced their budget, they put in hand all kinds of public works, and in 1933, as we have shown, conditions began rapidly to improve, though the improvement was delayed by a severe building strike.

How far was the rapid recovery from 1933 to 1935 due to the action of the Socialist Government? The best minds in Sweden are still debating this question; some hold that the recovery came naturally owing to the enterprise of the people, the recovery of the export trade, and other causes quite unconnected with the Government. Others hold that the expansionist policy of the Government did considerably accelerate the recovery, but admit that owing to the fact that the Government only came into power in 1932 they began their policy of public works too late, and that the unbalancing of the budget was on too small a scale to have much effect. But it remains true that they did deliberately unbalance the budget for the first three years they were in power, and then paid back the deficit during the boom years in accordance with their declared plan.

One interesting point is that " in 1933–34 and 1935–36 the Government had difficulty in persuading the administrators of state enterprises, who are not very different from private business men, to act in the interest of a countercycle. The railroads, for example, hesitated to order new equipment when their freights were falling off, but once started on the process of modernizing the railroads, the administrators did not want to stop in the middle, just as their business was picking up." [1]

Mr. Wigforss sums up the results of his own policy as follows: " The only question of practical importance is presented when it comes to deciding how the experience of past years should influence future action. If the question is put in this way, one ventures to say that a preponderant majority of the general public and of experts in these matters consider the experience so favorable that there should be future experimentation along the lines of ' the new fiscal policy '." [2]

This statement of Mr. Wigforss shows true Swedish moderation; in fact, it seems to me an understatement of

[1] *Fortune*, September 1938, p. 138.
[2] *Annals*, May 1938, p. 37.

what has been achieved. It is certainly in remarkable contrast with Mr. Dalton's view quoted at the beginning of this chapter!

I suggest that what has been done may be summed up as follows. The Socialist Government, at the bottom of the slump, declared its intention of departing from orthodox financial methods; during the slump it borrowed freely, deliberately unbalanced the budget, and did everything in its power to encourage spending, both by public and private authorities. When things improved it reduced public borrowing, kept up the taxes, repaid the budget deficit, and did everything possible to control public and private expenditure.[1] It almost certainly accelerated recovery and prevented the appearance of excessive boom conditions in 1937 and 1938. It has undoubtedly done a good deal to persuade the public in all parties that the counter cycle policy for unemployment is fundamentally sound.

PLANS FOR THE FUTURE

The really interesting question is how far the Swedish policy is likely to be effective in preventing depressions in the future. The Government is quite confident that its counter cycle policy is right, and it has gone far to convince almost everybody on that point, but its experience is limited to one rather long period (about six years) of steady recovery. It has learnt how difficult it is to regulate public and private expenditure sufficiently quickly and on a large enough scale to keep activity at a constant level. It is working hard to prepare plans for the future.

As regards public works, it is necessary to have a very large number of small jobs waiting to be done, with all preparations made. Large individual jobs take a long time to start, and once started cannot easily be stopped. Efforts are being made now through all the government organisations and through the local authorities to prepare masses of smallish jobs all over the country which can quickly be put into operation when conditions seem to

[1] *Swedish Liberal Economist :* " They did something but not as much as their programme. In particular, the restriction on public investment when good business conditions returned was too slow. They did little to prevent boom conditions in 1937 and 1938."

demand it. For instance, the city of Stockholm will shortly have a million pounds set aside for works of all kinds, which will not be put in hand until the Government gives the word. By way of contrast, it is interesting to note that in England it is still illegal for local authorities to build up reserve funds for any such purposes.

To quote Professor Myrdal: " Part of the preparation for crisis has been to take precautions in order to avoid delay in setting the spending program in motion. An intensive inventory of possible public works in the field of public buildings, road construction and municipal investments has thus been prepared. A general program for social housing has been worked out in some detail. The State production enterprises—railroads, power plants, post office system, mines, forest preserves, etc.—are urged to prepare yearly building programs for ten years in advance. They are asked to have available at all times technical and economic plans, ready for speedy action. The idea is that next crisis we shall not be caught unawares. The blue-prints shall be at hand, the measures shall be decided upon in advance, and the government shall have only to press the button to set the machinery in motion."

THE DOUBLE BUDGET

The basic feature of the Swedish counter cycle policy is that the budget must be balanced over a trade cycle as a whole, that there must be deficits in years of depression which must be made good by surpluses in boom years. It is important that the Government and public opinion should regard large budget deficits in slump years as normal and desirable. Mr. Wigforss has declared that he is planning to reduce taxation if a depression occurs, a thing that has never yet been done but which he considers undoubtedly right in principle. The problem is to carry out such novel and drastic steps without shaking public confidence and causing a flight of capital from the country.

The fact that the budget was deliberately unbalanced for about three years at the bottom of the last slump and that the deficit has now been paid back, must, of course, be the principal asset in securing public confidence. But the Swedish Government has adopted another device, which is intended to make plain to all that deficit budgets in times of slump are a normal part of Swedish economy. It has introduced a double budget, what Myrdal calls the running budget and the capital budget. " The running budget contains, on the one hand, receipts from taxation, the yearly profits from productive state enterprises and other yearly state incomes, and on the other side of the ledger, all sorts of ordinary expenditures which are not of the investment type, plus the writing-off of the ' productive ' investment. The capital budget, on the other hand, is regularly financed by borrowed money— insofar as free capital out of sinking funds in the different ' productive enterprises ' is not available; *i.e.*, insofar as the state is increasing investment over normal reinvestment."

The ingenious new idea which the Swedes have adopted is the adaptation of this method for all capital expenditure, including that which is non-reproductive. To quote Myrdal: " Thus, a public corporation, placed on the same level as the other productive enterprises of the state, was instituted to own and administer the state's public buildings, schools, post offices, hospitals, etc. The particular branch of administration has, thus, to pay to this corporation yearly rent for the use of its quarters. This rent is, of course, a yearly and ordinary expenditure on the running budget charged that particular branch of administration. The corporation, in its turn, utilizes its rent incomes for paying not only the upkeep of the buildings, but also interest and depreciation on the invested capital. The payment to the sinking fund is a matter of business routine and follows technical rules. This reform carries with it the added advantage of making the relative costs of different branches of public activity measurable and comparable with much more rationality and accuracy than was possible earlier when the various administrations were charged in the running budget with the costs of new buildings in the year, and only in the year, in which they happened to be built. In the present problem the reform means a greater flexibility in fiscal policy, because during a depression we can now expand our construction program for public buildings and finance it out of loans without breaking any budget principles and without endangering the 'soundness' of finances in the long run. The burden on the running budget is thus automatically kept upon the same level even for the years when the building program is shrinking."

This process is not yet completed, but Myrdal suggests that all capital expenditure should be dealt with on these lines.

Myrdal claims that this scheme has the advantages of flexibility and of soundness. Flexibility—because the system makes it seem just as sensible to borrow during a depression as during a boom: money can be borrowed and spent during the depression, when wages are low and contracting is cheap, and the main burden of paying interest and sinking fund can be borne during the boom, when the taxes can easily be carried. Soundness—because the open declaration of the intention to balance the budget only over a whole trade cycle should give the public confidence while deficits are being piled up in the slump.

So long as the sinking funds are adequate and the necessary taxation can be found to balance the running budget over a trade cycle, this whole process, according to Swedish authorities, should be both flexible and sound.

CAN FUTURE UNEMPLOYMENT BE PREVENTED?

How far is it likely that the experience the Swedish Government has gained in one depression and the plans it has made will enable it to avoid depressions in future?

Sweden is, of course, largely dependent on the export trade, and any sudden and severe reduction in the demand for exports will inevitably cause serious unemployment. At what rate it might be possible to absorb that unemployment in home industries it is difficult to foretell. And, as the figures previously quoted show, unemployment was abolished in 1930 under a non-Socialist government just as much as it was abolished in 1937 under the Socialist Government.

Experience of the counter cycle policy is so far limited to six or seven years. Those who believe in it most firmly are agreed that further experience is needed, and that in various ways the machinery for financial adjustment must be improved.

It has been pointed out that the managers even of the socialised sector of Swedish industry are for various reasons inclined to follow the ordinary cycle in their capital expenditure; a good deal of thought and energy must be devoted to training the managers to realise that it is in the national interest that they should follow a counter cycle policy; and that if this is done on a sufficiently large scale it will also be to the actual advantage of their particular undertaking.

To be wholly effective, it must be possible to control a considerable proportion of the total national expenditure so as to compensate for the rise and fall in private expenditure which seems bound to occur under the capitalist system.

Many people hold that the socialised sector, even if one includes everything controlled by the national government, local governments, and the co-operative societies, is too small to enable a counter cycle policy limited to that sector to be completely effective. Those who hold this view believe that ultimately a far larger proportion of Swedish industry must be socialised before trade fluctuations can be effectively and permanently prevented.[1]

However this may be, it is undoubtedly true that the problems of the trade cycle have been tackled by the Swedish Socialist Government with knowledge and vigour, and that they have certainly made some progress towards their solution. It can hardly be denied that what Sweden has done provides a lesson for the world in the use of controlled inflation. If the world continues to absorb Sweden's exports at fair prices, there would seem to be at least a reasonable possibility that the Swedish Government may be successful in avoiding serious depressions in the future.

[1] *Swedish Liberal Economist :* " Can one sufficiently control the volume of investment if one does not control the factor on which three-quarters of it—all private investment—depends, *i.e.,* costs? Can a trade-union Socialist Government control rising costs in good times? "

CHAPTER V

HOUSING AND TOWN PLANNING IN STOCKHOLM

I SPENT my first fortnight in Sweden studying the local government of Stockholm. After my experience in Switzerland I wanted to find out how far local government was responsible for the success of Swedish democracy. Frankly, I was disappointed; I came to the conclusion that local government in Stockholm was on about the same level as that in Manchester, that is to say, it is honest and fairly competent, without much energy or imagination; and there are few signs of any general or deeply felt sense of responsibility among the citizens for the government of their city.

I studied especially housing and town planning, partly because these were said to be particularly good, partly because they are the subjects which I know best, and I am printing my conclusions because they illustrate both some of the strong and some of the weak spots of Stockholm city government.

TOWN PLANNING

Stockholm is a beautiful city. It has been so often described that I will confine myself to a few quotations from Clough Williams-Ellis. He says a city ought to be a fit setting for a civilised life, and adds:—

" Sweden's capital seems to me to be such a setting, and indeed I myself put it above every other city whatsoever. . . . Stockholm has no squalor, no shameful hinder parts, and very little unnecessary ugliness whether industrial or other. . . .

" No one, I think, could visit the new Town Hall at

Stockholm without feeling that it proclaimed and made manifest, not only the just pride of the loveliest city in the world, but also the renaissance of its people.

"In it are employed and displayed and combined into one uplifting masterpiece all the fine and applied arts of modern Sweden—a great orchestral symphony conducted through a thousand intricate passages to a noble conclusion by its designer. . . .

"To discover a tract of the world in which the best architects and sculptors are popularly known and acclaimed as are Derby winners or Cup-tie players in England was a warming experience that, if it made me happier as a human being, certainly reduced my complacency as a Briton. . . .

"I shall try to visit Stockholm again this summer, secure in the knowledge that wherever my beloved Stockholm has been changed or extended, beauty and dignity will have been added."

That is a high testimonial from an authority who can be very critical. Nobody can deny that Stockholm deserves at least the greater part of this lavish praise.

Stockholm owes much to nature. The site is an ideal one; the city is built on islands surrounded by lakes and rivers. There are no other cities near at hand. Any amount of good building land is available, almost the whole of it covered by forests, which make a perfect setting for suburban development.

Further afield is the famous Stockholm archipelago, consisting of thousands of islands, ideal spots for summer houses or for expeditions during the weekend, or even in the long summer evenings.

But man has played his part too. Thanks to the waterfalls of Sweden, abundant and cheap electricity is available; the factories are all electrically driven and practically smokeless. The city as a whole is remarkably clean (though, for some reason, the small steamers are allowed to pour out volumes of black smoke right in the centre of the town).

Not only is Stockholm a city of beautiful surroundings and beautiful buildings, but the people are careful not to spoil it. Everything is clean. Disfiguring advertisements are so strictly controlled that they do little harm, and one rarely sees litter.

One can understand that nearly all visitors to the city share Clough Williams-Ellis's enthusiasm. It is a capital of which Sweden may well be proud, " a fit setting for a civilised life ".

This result is, of course, not achieved without thought and trouble. The Stockholm City Council takes town planning seriously. The whole of the development of the city is under the charge of one of the municipal ministers : town planning, land purchase, housing. It is his business to co-ordinate all these different sections. He is responsible for the harmonious and effective planning and development of the city. There is an important department of planning, with a highly skilled technical staff of town planners, architects, engineers, and surveyors, costing no less than £20,000 a year in salaries alone. Manchester, whose need for town planning is desperate, has no official staff of experienced town planners; the work is left to the overloaded staff of the City Surveyor.

Stockholm has grown rapidly in recent years, as the following table shows :—

TABLE I

Population of Stockholm

	Inner City	Suburbs	Total
1900 . . .	300,000	10,000	310,000
1910 . . .	342,000	22,000	364,000
1920 . . .	375,000	44,000	419,000
1930 . . .	427,000	75,000	502,000
1936 . . .	450,000	90,000	540,000

In 1900 the area of the city was 7,500 acres, consisting of what is now known as the Inner City. In 1913 and 1914 the present suburbs were added, with an area of 22,000 acres, so that the whole city now has an area of practically 30,000 acres. The population is 540,000, and with the additional persons living in the surrounding areas the total population of Greater Stockholm is about 700,000.

It is an old Swedish tradition that cities should purchase

and own considerable portions of the land on which they are built. The city of Stochkolm owns nearly one-third of the Inner City, much of which was purchased in the days of old. Since 1904 the City Council has been steadily purchasing land in the suburbs and even beyond. It now owns something like 80 per cent. of the suburban land, which, of course, enables it effectively to control the building development.

The Inner City is built in the usual Continental style. Apart from the fine buildings, such as the King's Palace, the Town Hall, and many other public buildings of all kinds, the dwellings consist mainly of six- to eight-storeyed buildings. Separate houses for single families are almost unknown.

The planning of the Inner City does not present points of any special interest from the English point of view. There is a fair supply of open spaces; traffic problems exist but are not serious; street widenings and an increased number of open spaces and playgrounds for children are desirable.

There is only one point of outstanding importance: the exceedingly high cost of land. Almost everybody wants to live in the Inner City; the development of offices and other business premises in the central square mile of the city has meant a reduction of the population in that area in recent years; but the population in the remainder of the Inner City has been increasing rapidly, as shown by Table I. The City Council has made efforts to induce people to live in the suburbs with some success; but the population of the Inner City has even in recent years been increasing twice as fast as the suburban population.

As the Inner City has an area of only 7,500 acres, land is becoming very scarce and land values are exceedingly high. Table II, for which I am indebted to the Statistical Department of the City of Stockholm, gives the principal facts.

The head of the department comments: " The separate value of land is not known before 1919. The value of land in per cent. of total value must have been higher in 1920 than in 1929, but can hardly have exceeded 40 per cent. This figure gives a land value in 1920 of about 940 mill. kr.; it can be regarded as a maximum figure of the land value in that year."

At the present time the prices being paid for land for the erection of blocks of flats in the outer part of the Inner City average something like £40,000 per acre; perhaps ten times as much as the price of land an equivalent distance from the centre in the larger city of Manchester.

This is the really serious planning problem for Stockholm. The high land values in the Inner City inevitably mean high buildings and high rents; as more and more expensive

TABLE II

Land in the Inner City

Year	Value of land, mill. kr.[1]	Value of buildings, mill. kr.	Value of land and buildings, mill. kr.	Value of land in per cent. of total value
1920	—	—	2,349	—
1929	1,269	2,261	3,530	36·0
1937	1,588	2,995	4,583	34·7

buildings are erected, land values continue to rise. Several Stockholm residents told me that they regarded the excessive cost of land and the speculation in land as the great scandals of Stockholm.

I was informed that about one-third of the Inner City is owned by the municipality, and one-third by the state. One might have thought that this large public ownership would have tended to keep prices down, but it seems to have no such effect. The various government and municipal departments regard it as their business to get full value for the land which they happen to own, and they are just as anxious to get the highest price as a private owner.

Coming to the suburbs, the position as regards land values is much better. On the one hand, there is almost unlimited land available, subject to the provision of adequate transport facilities; and on the other hand, the City Council owns something like 80 per cent. of the suburban land within the city.

The particular suburb which is being most rapidly developed at present is Bromma, which has an area of

[1] There are about 20 kronor to our pound.

5,000 acres and a population of 40,000 persons. It is planned to have an ultimate population of 100,000.

Bromma is being developed as a residence for persons who are working in Stockholm, not as a self-contained garden city, though there are a few factories in the northeast corner. The whole area is so beautifully wooded that many of the residents are satisfied with the natural beauties and have little or no formal garden.

Bromma is almost surrounded by broad straits and is connected with the city by a bridge, over which run buses and an electric train, by which it is possible to reach the centre of the city from the different parts of Bromma in from twenty to thirty minutes.

The best sites are those on the water front, which stretches for two or three miles on the south of the suburb; they are occupied by good-sized houses costing about £2,000 or £3,000. All the individual houses in Bromma are built of wood, but a large portion of the development, even in the suburbs, is in three-storeyed flats, especially as regards working-class houses.

Stockholm has been successful in inducing all classes to live in Bromma. It is estimated that the family incomes are approximately as follows:—

> 20% above £500 per annum;
> 30% from £250 to £500 per annum;
> 50% under £250 per annum.

Those under £250 per annum may be regarded as working class. But it must be recognised that no family with less than a regular income of about £180 per annum can live in Bromma and pay fares into Stockholm amounting, for one person, to about 3s. a week. It is, therefore, only the aristocracy of the working classes who can afford to live there.

There are, of course, the necessary schools, including a new secondary school, in Bromma, two cinemas, and two small churches; there is only one place at which drink is sold—the Aerodrome restaurant. Generally speaking, Bromma residents are expected to go into Stockholm for their amusements.

Not content with their large land purchases in the

suburbs, the City Council is anxious to purchase land right outside the city boundaries for holiday purposes. About a year ago they bought a beautifully wooded area—Tyresta —of about 3,000 acres, to be developed for camping and weekends. While I was in Stockholm the city purchased a large peninsular with no less than thirty-five miles of indented coast, also for holiday purposes. A large proportion of Stockholm citizens, including many of the working classes, own motor boats, and this new purchase, which is accessible from Stockholm in one hour by motor-boat or by motor-car, is intended to provide places for camping and picnicking for all those who want them.

Such, in very brief outline, are some of the main aspects of Stockholm town planning. There is only one serious difficulty—the high values of land in the centre. It is expected that Stockholm will continue to grow for some years. The town-planning department is working on the basis of an ultimate population of Stockholm of one million persons, and it is estimated that the number of families requiring separate dwellings will increase in much greater ratio than the population. It is likely, therefore, that land values will continue to increase.

There are two methods by which increasing land values might be avoided. The method which the City Council is pursuing is to develop surrounding areas by providing cheap and rapid transport. In this connection the City Council is seriously considering an underground railway. There is any amount of land ripe for development within a few miles of the centre, but as has already been pointed out development is still taking place slowly; apparently mainly because the residents prefer to live in the Inner City.

There would seem to be an alternative method of preventing increases of land values, or at least of securing the benefit of the increment for the community: the municipalisation of the whole of the land. In England the replanning of the central portions of the cities is almost entirely held up by the excessive demands for compensation. Many of us are being driven to the conclusion that the municipalisation of the whole of the land is an essential step towards the planning of beautiful and dignified and efficient cities.

Why should not the Stockholm City Council carry its traditional method of purchasing municipal land to its logical conclusion by municipalising the whole of the land within the city boundaries? This would no doubt be done by an Act of Parliament, handing over the ownership of the land to the City Council in return for land bonds at whatever might be considered to be a fair valuation.

Here is an opportunity for Stockholm to add to our debt to them. There is a Socialist majority on the Stockholm City Council and a Socialist Government in Sweden. In the city the Socialists have been in power for twenty years and have displayed that moderation and practical common sense for which Sweden is becoming famous in the world. May I suggest to the Stockholm City Council that they have a magnificent opportunity to be world pioneers in a piece of practical socialism? It is true that the land in the Inner City ought to have been municipalised thirty years ago. But immigration into Stockholm is still going on fast; it is generally agreed that the population, and still more the number of separate families, will continue to increase for some time. Land values will, therefore, grow even higher. If the whole of the land was nationalised at a fair price now, the City Council could, on the one hand, prevent land values and rents from rising any higher, and on the other hand, earn the necessary interest and sinking fund on their land investment, especially having regard to the fact that they are able to borrow long-term money for about 3 per cent. at the present time. This would, of course, give the City Council full control of the land in the Inner City. (The experiment would be even more interesting if they municipalised all buildings too, but this might be approaching a little too near to Moscow.) An experiment of this sort would set an exceedingly interesting and important example for the rest of the world.

In conclusion, may I endeavour to compare shortly what has been done in the way of town planning in Stockholm and my own city of Manchester?

In the first place Stockholm is a beautiful and, on the whole, well-planned city. Unfortunately, nobody can say the same of Manchester. Yet the Stockholm City Council is spending far more money, time, and thought on town planning than is being done in Manchester. That is the first lesson for Manchester: to inaugurate a strong and well-staffed, independent, town-planning department.

As regards the central areas of Stockholm and Manchester there is no comparison whatever. Stockholm is clean and fairly well planned, it has a large number of fine buildings, admirably situated. Manchester has many good buildings, but the whole central city is so crowded that none of them can be properly seen. Manchester could not hope to find a site for its town hall equal to or even approaching, in spacious beauty, that of Stockholm. But the congestion and the crowding in the centre of Manchester is surely unnecessary. Could Manchester not send its town-planning committee to spend a week in Stockholm and then consider what might be done in Manchester?

As regards suburbs, the comparison is by no means so unfavourable to Manchester. Bromma and Wythenshawe are both about the same size, are both being developed mainly as residential suburbs. Wythenshawe consists mainly of cottages for the working classes: so far as the design of the individual cottages and the planning of the estates is concerned, there can be no doubt that Wythenshawe is well ahead of Bromma. Bromma has rows of rather dreary, wooden, working-class houses that show up badly by comparison.

Bromma is by far the most attractive of the suburbs of Stockholm. The others seem to be developing as purely working-class areas, and do not offer attractions at all comparable to those of Bromma or Wythenshawe.

Undoubtedly the most interesting piece of planning in Stockholm from the point of view of Manchester is the purchase by Stockholm of large areas of well-wooded and watered country, ten or fifteen miles from the centre of the city. Manchester has the equally attractive Derbyshire hills within easy distance, but has so far never contemplated their acquisition. Why does the City Council not buy a few of the glorious mountains and valleys of Derbyshire, and run cheap 'bus services out to them at week-ends?

Stockholm is a beautiful, healthy, and convenient city. There are, of course, drawbacks, but on the whole it may fairly be said that nature and man have conspired together to make something approaching an ideal city: a city in

D

which it is the fault of the individual inhabitant if he does not live a pleasant and healthy life.

HOUSING

Stockholm has a population of 540,000 and no less than 180,000 separate dwellings.[1] The population has grown rapidly during the last twelve years; the number of dwellings even more rapidly, as the following table shows:—

	Dwellings	Population	Persons per dwelling
January 1st, 1925 . .	108,000	438,000	4
December 31st, 1936 .	180,000	540,000	3
Increase in 12 years .	72,000	102,000	—

During the last twelve years no less than 72,000 new dwellings have been built, or an average of 6,000 each year. Forty per cent. of the dwellings in Stockholm are less than twelve years old.

A City of Small Families

The growth of the population of Stockholm is due to immigration from the country, not to any natural increase. In fact, the number of children is distressingly small; the net reproduction rate is estimated to be between thirty and fifty—which means that apart from immigration the number of women of child-bearing age thirty years hence will be between 30 and 50 per cent. of the present number. The scarcity of children is shown strikingly by the following facts:—

1. The number of persons per dwelling is exactly 3.

2. There are only 70,000 children under sixteen in the whole city, out of a population of 540,000.

3. There are actually no children whatever in two-thirds of the houses in Stockholm.

4. One-half of the " families " living in separate dwellings in Stockholm consist of one single person.

[1] The word " dwelling " is used to include both flats and cottages.

The standard of living is good. It has been rising very rapidly, perhaps more rapidly than in any other European country during the last seventy years. In regard to incomes and purchasing power, Stockholm is now probably about equal to Manchester. Families in Stockholm are, however, substantially smaller than in Manchester, and they would seem to be able and willing to pay higher rents.

The Standard of Housing

The outstanding fact about Stockholm housing is the smallness of the individual dwelling. Half the dwellings in the city consist of one room and kitchen, or less; another quarter of two rooms and kitchen, leaving actually less than a quarter consisting of three rooms and kitchen, or more. The great bulk of the working-class families live either in one room and a kitchen or in a single room.

Separate living-rooms are almost unknown in working-class dwellings: I must have visited at least twenty without seeing a single bed. Much ingenuity has been displayed in designing sofas and armchairs which are turned into single and double beds at night. The " one-room-and-kitchen house " therefore is a living-room and kitchen by day and a bedroom and kitchen by night. Owing, on the one hand, to old custom, and, on the other hand, to the high rents, this seems to be very widely accepted, though, of course, doctors and reformers carry on a constant agitation in favour of larger houses. The oldest flat we visited was shown us by our taxi driver, who spontaneously offered to do so. It was built by the City Council in 1920, and consisted of one fairly large room for living and sleeping and a small kitchen. It was occupied by the chauffeur, his wife, and one child. The total area was 420 square feet; there was no bathroom; the only washing place was the sink in the kitchen. There was a w.c. in what was practically a dark, unventilated cupboard. The furniture was good, and the whole place beautifully tidy. The rent was no less than 16s. a week.

Another flat we visited was one built by the Housing Co-operative Society in 1932. It is in a big block of flats, in an excellent part of the city where development is still proceeding. It consists of three living-rooms with windows;

a kitchenette and a bathroom, neither of them with windows or ventilation to the open air, and a larder ventilated into an inner corridor. There is a glass partition between the kitchenette and the dining-room: central heating from September to May and hot water all the year round in the kitchen and bathroom. There is a lift, a rubbish shoot in the passage, a common room each for washing and carpet beating, and playroom and playground for children. The playroom is used as a gymnasium for the parents in the evenings. The area of the flat is 550 square feet, and the rent 30s. a week.

In England we had the advantage of a government committee, which produced an admirable report on working-class housing in 1918. They laid down that the minimum family house should contain the following: a living-room, a kitchen, three bedrooms, a bathroom and w.c.—all these rooms to have windows to the open air; a larder with ventilation to the north. The minimum floor area should be 750 square feet. These standards have been pretty well maintained for the whole of the three and a half million houses built since the war. It should be added that practically all these houses have a separate garden.

No such conditions were laid down in Stockholm, and back-to-back flats, with unventilated kitchens and lavatories are not only common, but are actually being built to-day. At the same time, the designs have been steadily improving. The fittings are generally good, particularly in the kitchens, which have usually a standard stainless-steel sink and a good gas cooker, and three or four fair-sized cupboards for the storage of food and crockery. The furniture is in most cases good.

Nearly all modern flats in Stockholm have central heating and very often hot water laid on; a rubbish shoot is common, and there is usually a laundry, frequently playgrounds, and occasionally a crèche.

To sum up, the working-class dwellings built in Stockholm since the war are much smaller than those built in England; usually not so well designed, but provided with good fittings, well furnished, and beautifully kept.

Self-erected Cottages

Stockholm is very proud of its self-erected cottages, which are sold to working men on special conditions described later. We visited one of these cottages. It was a wooden bungalow with two rooms and a kitchen—600 square feet of floor space. One important difference from English cottages is that owing to the very cold winter foundations must be deep, and for that reason there are always cellars under Stockholm cottages. This, of course, greatly increases the accommodation and the cost.

The ground floor contains one large and one small living-room, lobby, kitchen, and cupboards, with all fittings similar to those in the flats. The cellar consists of one large room, which may be used as a garage (with an inclined access) or as workshop and store. There is also a bath-room and copper and, in a separate room, the central-heating apparatus and store for coke. There is also a balcony and a garden of about 500 square yards.

The cottage we saw had excellent fittings and good furniture. With the help of the cellars there was plenty of room, though, as usual, there were only two rooms and a kitchen, and both living-rooms were used for sleeping purposes.

The estates on which these houses are built are laid out by the city. I saw a good many of them. In all cases the cottages are quite uniform, generally about ten feet apart, and built in straight rows. They are always single cottages. There is no relief to the monotony by building blocks of two or four. The whole arrangement is drab, unimagina-tive, and ugly, though in the older estates the trees and gardens, of course, make things rather better.

The cost of the cottage is £600, excluding the land, which is leased from the city. Annual payments purchase the cottage; 20s. a week for thirty years and 8s. a week for a continued mortgage thereafter. An English cottage of 750 square feet, equally well fitted and with a larger number of rooms, costs to-day about £350.

Rents

Rents in Stockholm are exceedingly high in comparison with those in Manchester. The statistics divide houses into those with and without central heating. The cost of central heating for a period of about nine months is included in the rent, which does not vary throughout the year. The difference between the average rents of those with and without central heating is, however, largely due to the fact that the house without central heating is, on the average, older and not so good as the one with it. The main facts are given in the following table:—

	Rent per Week of Houses with no C.H.		Rent per Week of Houses with C.H.	
	Inner City s.	Suburb s.	Inner City s.	Suburb s.
One room . . .	8	6	15	12
One room and kitchen .	12	10	20	19
Two rooms and kitchen .	18	13	30	27

The fairest comparison between rents in Stockholm and Manchester would seem to be to compare the Stockholm cottage built in the suburbs with two rooms and a kitchen and central heating, rented at 27s. a week, with the Manchester non-parlour, three-bedroom house, rented at 12s. a week (inclusive of rates). The comparison is shown by the following table:—

	Manchester	Stockholm
Size	750 square feet	600 square feet
Rooms	Four + kitchen	Two + kitchen
Rent	12s. per week	27s. per week

The rent of the Stockholm house, which is smaller and has fewer rooms than the Manchester house, is actually more than double the Manchester rent. It must be borne in mind that the Stockholm house includes central heating, and that the one in Manchester has received a subsidy of perhaps 5s. a week. The remainder of the difference is due to the higher cost of the Stockholm house.

These very high rents are the most serious feature of Stockholm housing, and are, of course, mainly responsible for the smallness of the houses. The chief reasons for the excessive costs in Stockholm (which are much higher than the rest of Sweden) are as follows:—

1. The climate renders necessary deep foundations, thicker walls and double windows, and central heating.

2. Actual cost of building is higher, owing to higher wages.

3. The cost of land in Stockholm is substantially higher than in Manchester, even in the suburbs.

4. The small size of the Stockholm flats increases the cost per square foot.

5. Stockholm flats may have rather more equipment in the way of cupboards, though it is doubtful whether this amounts to much.

Overcrowding

The contrast between Swedish and British views as to what constitutes overcrowding is vividly illustrated by the following quotation from an official publication of the Stockholm City Council.

" Loans are granted for the erection of dwellings of *at least two rooms and a kitchen for large families.*"

The idea that a highly civilised country like Sweden regards a flat of two rooms and a kitchen as adequate for a large family strikes anybody accustomed to English standards as amazing. We assume that there should always be a bedroom for the parents, another for the boys, and a third for the girls, as well as a living-room and kitchen. In other words, four rooms and a kitchen are regarded as the very minimum for a large family; whereas Stockholm is content with two rooms and a kitchen, which gives them two living-rooms by day and two bedrooms only at night.

Fortunately (from one point of view) the number of large families in Stockholm is very limited, as shown by the following table:—

	End of 1935 [1]			
	One room and kitchen	Two rooms and kitchen	Three or more rooms and kitchen	Total
Families with three children .	1,106	927	1,148	3,181
Families with three or more children .	431	443	359	1,233
	1,537	1,370	1,507	4,414

This shows that just under 3,000 of these large families are living in two rooms and a kitchen, or less.

The available statistics show that the overcrowding in Stockholm has become substantially less during the last twenty years, not because larger houses are being built, but because families have become very much smaller. About one-half of the " families " occupying separate flats in Stockholm to-day consist of one single person.

The following table shows the number of dwellings of different sizes in Stockholm in 1920 and 1937 respectively :—

	Number of dwellings	
	1920	1937
One room	14,000	29,000
One room and kitchen, or two rooms .	35,000	66,000
Two rooms and kitchen . . .	24,000	43,000
Larger	29,000	43,000
Totals . . .	102,000	181,000

This table shows that the proportion of dwellings in Stockholm not exceeding two rooms has actually increased in the last seventeen years from 48 to 52 per cent.; the

[1] From p. 104. *Statistical Year Book.*

number not exceeding three rooms has increased from 71 to 76 per cent.

Overcrowding is not widespread because the number of children is so small. But the large poor families are badly overcrowded; for instance, the official statistics record one case of five adults and five children living in a flat of one room and a kitchen. But there are so few poor large families that the number of overcrowding cases is not great.

A City Without Slums?

The civic authorities claim that there are practically no slums in Stockholm, and this is true in the sense that there is no district that looks outwardly like an English slum district. In all parts of the city the houses are clean and generally pleasant to look upon. On the other hand, there are many dwellings which we should consider unfit for human habitation. There are old houses in the Inner City, sometimes five or six storeys high, facing streets not more than eight or ten feet wide. The flats in the lower storeys of these houses get little light and hardly any ventilation.

The authorities say that there are two or three thousand dwellings which require reconstructing. Others hold that a far larger number should be swept away and rebuilt.

Slum clearance has not yet begun, with the exception of one experiment carried out by a public utility company, which has reconstructed an old block of flats in one of the worst areas, reducing the number of flats from seventy-five to fifty, and making an attractive grass court. Those in charge of the company are much interested in preserving the mediæval character of the district, and have succeeded in making some of the reconstructed flats very pleasant— so much so that many of the best of them are now occupied by artists and other professional workers. On the other hand, some of the reconstructed flats are dark and badly ventilated.

The city has granted a loan for this work, substantially larger than would have been granted on ordinary business terms, and is, therefore, taking some risk, but the promoters hope that in the end the whole thing will prove to be self-supporting. They are now endeavouring to raise funds from private sources and intend to tackle another block of flats in a similar manner. But the fact remains that Stockholm has hitherto dealt only with seventy-five of her slum flats.

Building by Private Enterprise

The great building activity of the last fifteen years has been substantially due to private enterprise. At least four-fifths of the dwellings, an average of perhaps 5,000 dwellings per annum, have been built by speculative builders. The vast majority of these dwellings are flats; on the whole they seem to be well built, and the quality of the fittings and accessories has constantly improved to meet the steadily rising demand for comfort and luxury.

The best working-class flats I saw were a group of 600 erected by a private builder in the last few years. They consisted of a series of simply- but well-designed three-storey flats, well laid out, with a children's playground and pleasant surroundings. There were six flats to each staircase; each flat was well planned, on the lines usual in England. Everything possible had been standardised; there was a laundry for each 200 flats. A flat of two rooms and a kitchen had an area of 500 square feet, cost £500, and was rented at 17s. a week.

My impression was that these working-class flats gave the best value for money of any unsubsidised flats I saw; probably better than anything built by the municipality or the co-operatives. Evidence in support of this conclusion was given by the fact that though the 600 flats had been occupied for over three years, there had been practically no removals; whereas in general the residents of Stockholm have the habit of constantly changing their homes.

Municipal Activity

The municipality, of course, makes the necessary bye-laws to regulate building and enforces them, as usual, through its inspectors.

During the inflation period of 1918–23 there was, as in other countries, an acute shortage of houses and a rise in rents. Sweden had her Rent Restriction Acts and the municipality during this period undertook a certain amount of subsidy building. Normal conditions returned much more quickly than in England. The Rent Restriction Acts were repealed in 1923 and municipal building came to an end. It was an unimportant episode in the history of Stockholm house building.

Municipal Loans

The municipality has constantly encouraged the owner-ship of houses by advancing loans at low rates, approximately at cost to the municipality. The municipality can, at present, borrow at about 2·7 per cent. for long periods. In general it borrows money as cheaply as the state.

The total housing loans outstanding at present amount to about three millions pounds. There is, of course, some risk in connection with these loans, but this is generally held to be very slight.

Self-erected Houses

The municipality has for many years endeavoured to encourage the building of separate cottages in the suburbs. In recent years it has developed the following rather original method of dealing with this problem.

Certain standard types of cottages have been worked out, one of which has been previously described. Three cottages of different types have been erected and these are open to inspection by anybody desiring to build his own house.

The prospective owner has to deposit £15. He chooses and rents a site belonging to the municipality already provided with roads and sewers, and proceeds to erect his own house with the help, and under the supervision, of the municipality.

So far as possible, everything is " pre-fabricated "—that is to say, supplied in such a way that it can be fitted together by unskilled labour. Where skilled labour is required it is provided by the municipality.

It is estimated that about a thousand hours of work, worth about £50, have to be provided by the owner. This is a heavy task as the house has to be erected during the summer months. It means fifty hours' work a week for twenty weeks, and even though the owner generally gets a good deal of help from friends, it is a task hardly likely to be undertaken except by a strong, active, and energetic man. It is no doubt partly for this reason that, although the scheme is working well, there have only been 3,000 houses erected in the last ten years, and the programme for the current year is limited to 400 houses.

On the other hand, the building of his own house by the owner undoubtedly causes him and his family to take great pride in the house, and should certainly help him to understand how to keep it in first-class repair.

This seems an admirable piece of initiative on the part of the municipality. One could only wish that their programme for next year included 4,000 houses instead of 400, and that a little more variety could be introduced, both into the planning of the estates and the external appearance of the houses.

The Poor Large Family

The most difficult problem in connection with working-class housing is always the housing of families with small incomes and several children. As we have already shown, Stockholm is (in one sense) fortunate in this matter, because it has very few large families.

Nothing effective was done in this matter until 1935, when Parliament passed an Act to give subsidies to poor families with three or more children. It was made a condition that the city should give the site free of charge and that dwellings should not be smaller than two rooms and a kitchen. Further, the city must provide certain amenities, such as playgrounds for the children.

The Government is prepared to give a grant equal to 30 per cent. of the rent for three children under sixteen, 40 per cent. for four, and 50 per cent. for five children, for families below a certain income limit, which works out for a family of two parents and three dependent children at 70s. a week. The Riksdag has this year amended the Act by allowing a grant up to 60 per cent. for six and seven, and 70 per cent. for eight or more children.

Stockholm has built 1,250 such flats in the last two or three years, and provided playgrounds and a few crèches. The houses are not built directly by the municipality, but through a specially created, non-profit-making company, or through one of the co-operative societies.

As the number of poor large families is so limited, it is hoped that suitable houses can be provided for them all under this scheme within five years.

The gross rent of a two-room-plus-kitchen flat under this scheme is about 15s. a week. When the three-children subsidy is allowed it comes down to 10s. a week. I found a case of a carpenter, with an income of £200 a year, renting one of these flats with five rooms and a kitchen to accommodate himself, his wife, and six children. The normal rent of the flat was 36s.; thanks to the 50 per cent. subsidy, he was paying 18s.; even this seems to us in England a very heavy rent for an artisan.

Cost to the Municipality

The municipality gives no direct cash subsidies for housing. The housing loans involve a certain risk but no actual charge in the budget.

The only annual charge is in connection with the free or cheap sites provided in certain cases. I did not succeed in getting any figure to indicate the total cost to the municipality, but it is certainly not a heavy charge.

The Building Co-operatives

A number of co-operative societies have grown up in the last twenty years. A number of individuals who want to build their own flats unite together in order to build them co-operatively. The most famous of these house-building co-operatives, H.S.B., is on a considerable scale; it has a headquarters staff of over 400 persons, and employs experts in every aspect of housing, including the provision of furniture and fittings. The co-operatives claim that they work without profit for the benefit of their members; that the scale on which they work enables them to carry out the technical work, to purchase the materials, and to build the houses more cheaply than these operations could otherwise be carried out. In particular, they claim that they borrow capital on cheap terms, and that their rents are substantially less than the rents of equivalent private flats.

Further, they claim that by fixing rents at a reasonable level they prevent the whole rent level from rising, and in particular prevent private enterprise from demanding excessive rents at times when there is a housing shortage.

The quality of the houses built by H.S.B. is probably better than the average private-enterprise house, and the houses seem to be generally popular. It is surprising to an Englishman that H.S.B. is still building houses containing lavatories and kitchens without windows, and not directly ventilated to the open air.

During the last fifteen years the housing co-operatives have built about 10,000 houses; which is about 12 per cent. of the total new houses built.

Flats or Cottages

The most striking contrast between the housing of the working classes in Stockholm and in Manchester is that in Stockholm well over 90 per cent. live in flats, whereas in Manchester nearly 100 per cent. live in separate houses.

In Stockholm, till recently, individual houses have been built only for the rich. Now there are several thousand cottages occupied by the élite of the working classes in the suburbs of Stockholm, but the great bulk of the population still prefer flats. The reasons for this may be summed up shortly as follows :—

1. *Custom.* Just as it has never occurred to the ordinary Manchester family that life in a flat is conceivable, so the idea of a separate cottage is a surprising innovation to the ordinary Stockholm worker.

2. There are no cheap cottages in Stockholm. The lowest rent is about 18s. a week, to which must be added 3s. a week for each travelling member of the family and the extra cost of lunching away from home.

3. In England one of the main reasons for preferring a cottage is the garden. But, owing to the severe and prolonged winter, the garden in Stockholm is worth much less than in Manchester. In fact, the Swedes, even in the country, do not cultivate their gardens with the same interest as is done in England.

4. I have already pointed out that no less than one-half of the families in Stockholm consist of a single person, and a considerable further number of two persons only. It is estimated that about 90 per cent. of the women in Stockholm continue to work on marriage and only gradually give it up as they grow older or have

children. The real advantage of a cottage is for the old-fashioned family, where the mother's chief interest is in her household and in her children. The old-fashioned family is apparently becoming a rare thing in Stockholm.

5. The size and plan of Stockholm are such that it is easy for the worker living in a central flat to get out to parks or to the country in the evenings and at weekends.

The whole idea of cottages for the urban industrial working class is new in Sweden, and although it is being encouraged by the City Council it seems likely for all these reasons to develop rather slowly.

Working-Class Housing in Stockholm and Manchester

There is a striking contrast between working-class houses in Stockholm and in Manchester.

In Manchester the City Council has felt ever since the war that private enterprise was not able to build houses of an acceptable standard at rents low enough for the working classes to pay. The city has itself, therefore, steadily built working-class houses with a subsidy paid partly by the state and partly by the city, averaging about 5s. a week on the rent. The city has built about 30,000 such houses; on the average they have four rooms and a kitchen each, the floor area is 750 square feet, and the net rent 10s. a week. They are practically all cottages in suburban districts, each standing in its own garden, situated in a well laid out and pleasant estate. The houses are well designed internally and externally. These 30,000 houses represent undoubtedly the best standard of working-class housing which has yet been achieved, and the rents of those built during the last few years under the Slum Clearance Act are within the means of even the poorest workers.

On the other hand, the Stockholm City Council has left the housing of the workers almost entirely to private enterprise; large numbers of houses have been built for the working classes, almost all of them consisting of one or two rooms and a kitchen; the average area is about 500 square feet, and the rent about £1 a week.

The direct building of houses by the City Council, available at reasonable rents for the working classes, is limited to about 1,250 flats built with the help of a government subsidy during the last two or three years.

It is a remarkable paradox that the conservative Manchester City Council, stimulated by national governments which have been conservative for 80 per cent. of the period since the war, has devoted immense energy and large sums of money to building good working-class houses, to let at low rents, while the Stockholm City Council, for twenty years under socialist control, with a socialist national government for a considerable portion of the period, has made no comparable effort to deal with the housing needs of the workers.

And although, as I have shown, Stockholm is doing far more effective work in town planning than Manchester, yet in the design and building of working-class houses and housing estates Manchester is far ahead of Stockholm.

Having made this comparison to the disadvatage of Stockholm, it must at once be admitted that not only has Manchester a far larger number of poor large families than Stockholm, but that the slums in Manchester are so much worse, and, above all, so much more obvious than any bad housing existing in Stockholm, that the public conscience in Manchester has naturally been more deeply stirred and has made more insistent demands for reform than has been the case in Stockholm.

Finally, let me add, lest any Manchester reader should feel unduly complacent, that while the infant death rate in Manchester is 70, in Stockholm it is only 28, so that the small dwellings of Stockholm and the habit of sleeping in the living-room do not seem to have any disastrous effect on the health of the occupants.

APPENDIX

The following letter from a very able and experienced Stockholm administrator, with unusual powers of looking objectively at his own familiar affairs, may help the reader to form a better picture of Stockholm housing and planning.

" You have given a very high appreciation of Stockholm, its nature and architecture, and it is, of course, impossible for me as a citizen of Stockholm to disagree. It is an everyday experience for us, but, notwithstanding, I think it is something quite exceptional to take in the natural freshness of this city of ours and the solemn, moving beauty, every morning new, of our town hall. All the same, the shadows are sufficiently deep and I cannot evade the impression that your description, although you have seen defects which most foreigners do not observe, is too light and too friendly.

" It is true we have no slums in the English sense, but you must always remember when you look at this question in Stockholm, that a very great part of the population, according to the last census 70 per cent., lives in flats with only two rooms and a kitchen (or less), and that the rent for the standard dwellings of one room and a kitchen amounts to about 1,030 kronor, *i.e.*, certainly more than 25 per cent. of the average family income. The economic burden of the bad housing conditions lies, accordingly, very heavily on our population.

" I think the root of the evil is to be found in the scarcity of building land during the last decades. The land values have risen much faster in the last few years owing to the low interest on capital; the decrease in the rents which might have been expected as a consequence of the decrease in the interest from 5 to $2\frac{1}{2}$–3 per cent. on first-class mortgage has failed to appear and has been replaced by a rapid rise in land values, which at the present moment are certainly much higher than your figures indicate. As a matter of fact, it pays to buy estates with buildings, thirty to forty years old, in rather good condition, to pull them down and erect new and modern ones in their place.

" According to our legislation the municipality is responsible for the expansion of the city and these exceptional conditions are, consequently, the result of shortcomings in the municipal administration. In the first place, and above all, I consider that the municipality has neglected to prepare long-termed expansion plans for the building of streets and arranging the building plots in depression as well as in rush days. As a matter of fact, we have, as we say in Swedish, the whole time been ' eating from hand to mouth '—we have prepared far too small areas and we always lag behind the demand in rush times. As nature has fashioned the Stockholm topography we would have needed many more bridges and arterial roads to the outskirts at a much earlier date than when we got them.

" Further, I think you are right in your idea about a municipalisation of the land in the Inner City. As a matter of course we ought to have bought everything we could have acquired for a reasonable price in the Inner City during the last twenty years. Such measures would have given us freedom in the replanning of the city which, so far, is still lacking and prevents us from rebuilding it as it ought to be rebuilt to function in the proper way under new conditions. This mistake can, however, not be remedied by appropriation, as present values would be far too high and the prices, being on the top, too risky.

" It is true that the Swedish population and Swedish politics may boast of a certain moderation and practical common sense. We have a certain sense for order, justice, moderation—but I sometimes ask myself if we do not lack the capacity of being captivated by genius and broad idealism. I have a suspicion that this feature of our national character has deepened as we have developed from a big to a small power during the course of history, just as the Swiss may be characterised, they say, by somewhat *bourgeois* features: prudence and security."

CHAPTER VI

DENMARK: A CO-OPERATIVE COMMONWEALTH

DENMARK is naturally a poor country. The land is low and flat; the agricultural land is of moderate quality, hardly any of it very good; up to a short time ago a large part of the peninsula of Jutland was barren heath. There are no considerable rivers, no minerals, no water power, and almost no forests.

Denmark has a population of 3,700,000 crowded into a small country at the rate of 237 per square mile, as against Sweden's thirty-five per square mile. She is fortunate in having no substantial minorities, either racial or religious, though she has a small, but to-day very dangerous, minority of Germans in Schleswig.

In spite of the natural poverty of their country, the people of Denmark have achieved for themselves a high standard of living: they have shown outstanding efficiency both in agriculture and in industry.

Perhaps the most successful piece of economic planning in any democracy is the peaceful agricultural revolution carried through by the farmers of Denmark since 1870. It is all the more remarkable because its success was not due to the initiative of a Coke of Norfolk or to the lead of any large farmer, but to the almost spontaneous growth of co-operation and of scientific farming among the mass of small holders, led by farmers who had been stimulated by the educational work of Grundtvig. Farming in Denmark is perhaps the world's outstanding example of effective planning by very large numbers of separate owners.

Prior to the Napoleonic Wars Denmark was a nation of substantial importance in the affairs of Europe; Norway formed part of the kingdom up to 1814. The Napoleonic Wars were disastrous; the Danish fleet was destroyed by

the British in 1807 at the Battle of Copenhagen; in 1814
Denmark lost Norway; in 1864 she lost Schleswig-Holstein
to Germany. On the top of these political losses came
serious economic trouble. Denmark was mainly a wheat-
growing country; in the 1870's Europe was flooded with
cheap corn from the virgin lands of America and Australia;
wheat fell to nearly half the price it had commanded in
the '60s, bringing disaster to European agriculture. It was
met by different countries in different ways. England did
nothing; with the result that English agriculture suffered
a terrible setback and did not begin to recover until about
1896. Germany saved its agriculture by protection.
Denmark took an entirely different course; it took advantage of the low price of wheat and the relatively good prices
of bacon and butter to swing its whole agricultural system
over to that of arable animal husbandry: the farmers
continued to grow cereals, but instead of selling them, fed
them to animals and sold the product mainly as butter or
bacon, which require a higher degree of skill and scientific
management for efficient production.

This policy was pursued with steady and increasing
success. There is general agreement that this success was
due mainly to the adoption of the co-operative system.
The world's first co-operative dairy was founded in Denmark in 1882. They soon sprang up all over the country;
to-day there are no less than 1400 of them in Denmark.

" The change in the style of farming began about
1875. At that time England was buying her butter,
eggs and bacon from Ireland. The Danes sent a commission to the latter country to learn how the Irish
produced these things. Then they set to work to win the
British market for themselves. Soon Denmark was
producing better bacon, better butter, better eggs than
the Irish. In recent years no less than four special
commissions have been sent to Denmark from Ireland
and Scotland to find out how it is done." [1]

It may be easier to understand the achievements of
Danish co-operation if I begin by describing a typical
co-operative dairy which I visited; it is neither one of the
most modern, nor by any means one of the largest.

[1] *Denmark : The Co-operative Way*, by F. C. Howe, p. 35.

A Co-operative Dairy

This dairy has 145 members living within a distance of not more than five or six miles. Their holdings vary from a few acres up to about fifty. Their main product is milk, though most of them also have a few pigs. They have between them 1,100 cows in milk, an average of less than eight for each farm.

When we arrived the morning milk was being delivered at the dairy. It arrives in a cheap, but effective, cart, drawn by two horses, specially designed to hold about one and a half tons of milk in churns. Each cart collects the milk from about fifteen farms; they are accurately timed to arrive in rotation at intervals of about a quarter of an hour. There is almost no waiting, immediately on arrival the milk is unloaded. When that is finished, they begin to load the skimmed milk, which is invariably taken back to the farmers as feed for the pigs. Within half an hour the cart is off again to distribute the skimmed milk to the farmers.

A number of the peasants take contracts for the transport of milk, the earnings from which they regard as extra income. The whole transport system is a good example of Danish agricultural co-operative efficiency; it is difficult to see how it could be done more economically.

The milk is unloaded from the cart on to a platform which is at the same level as the bottom of the cart, and poured straight into a convenient receptacle, large enough to hold the whole of the milk of the average farmer. This receptacle is part of a weighing machine, which automatically records the weight of the milk as it is poured in. A sample is taken from each farmer's milk and put into one of 145 small bottles, one for each member, standing on a tray within easy reach. From these samples the percentage of butter fat is determined, on the basis of which the milk is paid for. Once a week a further sample is taken and tested for cleanliness.

The great bulk of the milk is converted into butter; a small portion is pasteurised and sold as whole milk; under certain conditions of the market cheese is manufactured. The Danes have taken up the manufacture of different kinds of cheese in recent years with their usual scientific thoroughness, and make excellent cheese of all kinds. In particular, they make a Camembert, which has a flavour equal to the best French Camembert, but is ahead of the French in having no skin and being always in perfect condition. I found it one of the chief attractions of the Danish dinner! They have succeeded in building up an export trade in Gorgonzola to Italy and in Camembert to France.

One interesting point is that the milk is divided into four grades according to its cleanliness, and that the price paid to the farmer varies by about 5 per cent. according to the degree of cleanness. This provides considerable incentive to the farmer to adopt clean methods, and particularly to cool the milk immediately after milking.

It is not necessary to describe the machinery. It seemed to be admirably adapted to its purpose, efficient, and economical. The whole installation gave the impression of being run on competent businesslike lines. Perhaps the most striking point was the scientific spirit which permeated the place. Everybody was constantly concerned with quantities and temperatures and tests and records. Every worker in the dairy is educated by daily practice to develop a scientific habit of mind.

The management of the dairy is very democratic. The annual meeting of the 145 farmers appoints a small committee of management; whether a farmer has one cow or fifty, he only gets a single vote, on the principle that " it is the men who vote, not the cows ". This committee in turn appoints an expert manager, who gets a salary of about £300 per annum and a pleasant house close to the factory.

The co-operative dairy is a member both of a regional and a national co-operative society; these larger societies exist for common purposes, such as advice, guidance, publicity, and the mangement of the export trade. They have no control whatever over the individual co-operative society, which is completely free and self-governing. Nor is there any control by legislation, except for the purpose of ensuring the constant high quality of Danish butter for export.

A SMALL HOLDER

We visited one of the small holders who is a member of the dairy. He had a farm of twelve acres of arable land; all in perfect order and intensively cultivated. He had three cows in milk. After we had inspected the farm, he produced a book showing, for each cow and for each month during the milking period, the yield of milk, the percentage of butter fat, and the quantity of each of five kinds of food given to the cow. These are recorded by an employee of a separate co-operative society, who visits the farm once a month, takes all the records, and enters them in a book. It has been found by experiment that one visit a month gives a sufficiently accurate record of the whole milking period. At the end of the milking period the book shows how much milk the cow has given, how much butter fat, and how much food of each kind it has consumed.

This provides the information on which an expert from another co-operative society advises the farmer on the right food for his cattle, and how to get the best results from all points of view.

The small holder showed us this book with great pride, and we were much impressed to find that each of his three cows had given nearly a thousand gallons in the last milking period. This is an exceedingly high yield; a great tribute to the result of the scientific methods employed.

The printed balance sheet of the co-operative dairy for the six months ending April 30th, 1938, showed that the milk was being sold at 6*d*. a gallon at the farm, and the skimmed milk charged back to the farmer at 1½*d*. a gallon.

The small holder was living on the product of twelve acres of average land and selling his milk at these very low prices. It is a remarkable tribute to the efficiency of his farming that he had a pleasant, beautifully kept house, was an active leader in various co-operative societies, and was clearly leading a full and varied and interesting life.

THE EXTENT OF CO-OPERATION

There are 205,000 farmers in Denmark, of whom 94 per cent. own their own farms. The size of the farms as given in the 1933 census is as follows:—

Size of farm	Number of farms	Proportion of land
Less than 7½ acres . .	28,000 or 14% ⎫	One-sixth
From 7½ to 25 acres . .	78,000 or 38% ⎭	
From 25 to 150 acres . .	94,000 or 46%	Two-thirds
Over 150 acres . . .	5,000 or 2%	One-sixth
	205,000	

"The co-operative movement is the most pervasive thing in the country. It is of the very texture of the average farmer's life. Through the co-operatives he performs for himself almost all of the functions that in other countries are performed by others for him. He assembles his milk and makes and markets his own butter and cheese. He kills his own hogs in his own slaughter-house and sells them in London through his own export agency. His agents collect his eggs and bring them to his own egg export society where they are candled, graded and made ready for shipment to a foreign market.

"He buys food for his cattle in distant lands as well as agricultural machinery, fertilizer and seeds. He manages his own banking in his own locality and establishes his own credit. Through mutual societies he insures his house and his livestock. He maintains breeding societies of pedigreed hogs, cattle and horses and controls societies as to all of his products.

"As a consumer he buys at wholesale and sells to himself at retail. He manufactures many things in his own factory and in co-operation with other Scandinavian countries, he maintains an international wholesale purchasing agency." [1]

"The wonderful system of co-operation in Danish agriculture in the highly developed form in which we find it now, embraces almost every branch of agriculture and agricultural industry, and has its ramifications in practically every parish in Denmark. It has built up an organisation so complete that all the threads converge to one point from which the joint action of the whole system is in a certain measure controlled. The co-operative movement in Danish agriculture was not

[1] *Denmark: The Co-operative Way*, F. C. Howe, pp. 61-2.

started by a circle of philanthropists or even by the landlords for the purpose of benefiting the practical farmers.
It has grown up locally and gradually among the
peasants in the villages, and takes its root in the feeling
of solidarity and a sense of the benefits of mutual help
among the peasants which can be traced back to remote
centuries." [1]

In 1933 there were nearly 8,000 co-operative societies of
all types in the country, of which over 5,000 were agricultural producers' societies and 1,800 consumers' societies.

The membership in all these societies was 1,662,962, out
of a total population of 3,550,656. In other words, every
average family of four persons was a member of approximately two societies.

The membership of the agricultural producers' co-
operatives in 1935 is given in the following table: [2]—

	Local societies	Membership
Co-operative dairies . . .	1,404	190,000
,, bacon factories . .	60	187,000
Egg-collecting centres . .	800	50,000
Cattle export societies . .	12	11,000
Feeding-stuff societies . .	1,434	92,000
Co-operative fertilizer societies .	1,484	55,000

The extent of the co-operative societies and the variety
of the work they perform is so amazing that it seems worth
while to analyse their objects under the following five heads.

1. Co-operatives for manufacture and sale. These co-
operatives collect the products from the farms, treat them
in any way that may be necessary, and arrange for their sale
at home or abroad. The main co-operatives coming
under this heading deal with milk, eggs, and bacon.

These selling co-operatives give a good deal of scientific
advice to their members on the quality of the products.
For instance, the dairies advise on the quality of milk, the
bacon co-operatives on the best breeding sows.

[1] *Co-operation in Danish Agriculture*, Faber, p. ix.
[2] *Denmark*, 1937, p. 78.

2. Purchase co-operatives. There are co-operatives for the purchase of seeds, fertilisers, of machinery and of feeding stuffs.

3. Credit co-operatives have gone far towards replacing private banks.

4. Co-operatives of scientific research and advice, whose main function is advice on some special subject, *e.g.*, improving the breeds of boars or bulls, improving the quality of the seed, supervising the feeding and care of cattle or other stock.

5. The usual consumers' co-operatives for household goods.

It is no exaggeration to say that the remarkable scientific nature of Danish farming is wholly due, directly or indirectly, to the co-operative system, and that almost the whole of the buying and selling for the farmers is done by the co-operatives. Private merchants exist to some extent both in buying and selling, but the co-operatives are so strong that the merchants can only continue by giving specially good services at economical prices. Anything in the nature of a ring against the farmers is rendered quite impossible by the efficiency and scope of the co-operative organisation.

Ownership

Soon after the co-operatives were founded the peasants began to agitate for ownership. A tenant had little interest in improving the property; he exhausted the soil; he had little prospect of establishing himself on a permanent and prosperous basis. The farmers set to work to get rid of tenancy. They became steadily more powerful in Parliament, which they almost controlled between 1900 and 1920. They made great progress through Acts of Parliament of different kinds, mainly by taxation of the large landlord on the one hand and loans to the peasant on the other, in increasing peasant ownership, and established it on a satisfactory basis. As above stated, 94 per cent. of the farms of Denmark are to-day worked by the owner.

Ownership of small farms has been made practicable and profitable only by the co-operative societies. The small man gets exactly the same prices for his milk, eggs, and bacon as the large man. All he has to do in connection with the sale of the whole of his produce is to join the appropriate co-operative society, and unless he wishes he need not do more than attend a meeting once a year. Everything else is done for him and done as efficiently and as economically as it can be done for the largest farmer.

And, of course, ownership means that the peasant and his family put their whole heart and soul into their tasks, and work the land as only an owner can and will do it, at the same time preserving and increasing its fertility to the best of their ability. They work all day during the summer; they have plenty of leisure during the winter for amusement and culture. Everybody who knows the Danish peasant bears witness to his high quality and self-respect.

Achievements of Danish Agriculture

Sir John Russell speaks of " The prodigious effect that combination of effort by the whole body of producers can exert in increasing output, in cheapening cost of production, in improving the quality and value of the produce, and in ameliorating the lot of the labourer ".[1] That the word " prodigious " is not exaggerated is perhaps best indicated by the following table:—

	Number of cows	Average per cow.		Total Butter fat, million lbs.
		Milk, lbs.	Butter fat, lbs.	
1861 . .	757,000	2,200	65	49
1930 . .	1,632,000	7,300	272	444

This table shows that since 1861 the number of cows in Denmark has doubled, the average yield of milk from each cow has more than trebled; and the percentage of butter fat in the milk has increased, so that each cow is now giving four times as much butter as in 1861, and the total amount of butter fat produced in the country is nine times as great.

[1] *Co-operation in Danish Agriculture*, Faber, p. vii.

Perhaps the most striking proof of the efficiency of Danish farming is the price at which they are able to produce milk.

The balance sheet of the co-operative dairy which I visited showed that in the winter of 1937–8 the price of milk at the farm was 6d. a gallon. I was assured by competent authorities that this could be taken as a fair average figure for the period. The average cost of milk production in England and Wales, as judged by costings on nearly 500 farms worked out by the Oxford Agricultural Economics Research Institute, was in the year 1935–6 (the latest figures available) between 9d. and 10d. on the farm, without allowance for interest on capital and charges for management; the total cost must certainly have been over 10d. So that the selling price of the Danish farmer, which must, of course, include all his costs and any profit, was less than 60 per cent. of the average English farm's cost.

QUALITY

The co-operative societies are also responsible for improvement in the quality of the product. They realised from the beginning that in order to obtain the best price, high quality and absolute reliability were essential. The following example will show how adaptable and quick they have been in adopting new methods. In 1891, it was discovered in Denmark that the flavour of the butter could be improved and made more regular by pasteurising the cream. This was rather a technical process, involving expensive machinery and more highly skilled scientific control than had previously been available. But the dairies which had installed this new pasteurising system constantly won the prizes at the agricultural shows, and in spite of what is generally regarded as the natural conservatism of farmers, this new system spread so rapidly that within six years practically the whole of the co-operative dairies had introduced it. As soon as the great majority of farmers were convinced of the value of the process, the government was ready to help, and introduced legislation insisting on the pasteurisation of all milk used in the manufacture of butter. Denmark was the first country to legislate for the special purpose of ensuring the constant high quality of butter, and the result of these scientific efforts by all concerned, peasants, co-operatives, and government, has been successfully to maintain the high quality of Danish butter on the British market, and so to secure the best prices.

BACON CO-OPERATIVES

The bacon co-operatives have also been very successful in the manufacture and marketing of bacon, in improving the breed of pig, and in many other ways. The pigs are fed cheaply on grain and on the skimmed milk returned from the dairies; the success of the pig industry is therefore in one sense a by-product of the co-operative dairies. The bacon factories are more elaborate than the dairies, and in order to be economical have to be on a larger scale. For instance, one bacon factory we inspected had 6,000 members, covering the whole northern section of Zeeland, some of the members living as far away as thirty miles. The factory was well organised and equipped with Danish machinery, though inevitably suffering from under-production in view of the recent drop in the export trade.

One interesting point about this co-operative was the evidence it gave that the Danish farmers understand democracy in the sense that they are prepared to delegate their authority to responsible leaders, and that the rank and file do not wish to interfere with the day-to-day management. About 1,000 of the 6,000 members usually attend the annual meeting; they elect a board of twenty-one, which meets quarterly. This board in its turn elects an executive of four, which meets monthly and is in close contact with the director, who is paid what is for Denmark the very high salary of nearly £1,000 a year. The director has a great deal of freedom and responsibility; but full reports are constantly made to the executive, through them to the board, and at the annual meeting to the members. The administration is similar to that in an ordinary limited company, and probably about equally efficient. There is, of course, the great difference that nobody makes a profit; any surplus on trading is returned to the individual farmers in proportion to the value of the pigs they supply.

An outstanding instance of the genius of Danish agriculture for planning and co-operation has recently been given in connection with the reduction in the number of pigs killed for the British market, which was suddenly cut down to less than half owing to the imposition of the British quota. There are few things more difficult in a capitalist industry than to face a sudden reduction of output; the result is usually desperate competition and ruin; and an industry consisting of 205,000 separate producing units would seem to present this problem in its most acute form. It has, however, been successfully solved by a complicated system of cards imposed compulsorily by the government in full agreement with the co-operatives and the farmers, under which the full price for a pig can only be obtained when the pig is accompanied by a card. There are many difficulties; it is impossible to find any formula under which the cards can be allotted that does not cause injustice, but on the whole it has worked admirably; the farmers know exactly how many pigs they can sell; they breed only the right number; and prices have been maintained.

EXPORTS

Much of the success of the Danish agricultural system is due to the fact that the farmers are producing only three commodities for export: pigs, milk, and eggs, and that all of these have to travel out of the country from two or three ports; so that bulk transactions are essential. This has the advantage of rendering grading easy. On the other hand, the success of the whole scheme turns on finding markets for these three exports; until recently this presented no difficulty—we in Britain took the products because of their high quality and moderate price. Three-quarters of the Danish exports consist of agricultural products; over half of the total exports go to Great Britain. The position is precarious owing to the Ottawa agreement and the strong tendency to give preference to the British Dominions, which have become very keen competitors of Denmark.

Danes sometimes point out that they are selling us about

fifteen million pounds worth of butter each year at 1s. a pound, which would cost us 2s. to make ourselves. They are saving us fifteen million pounds in providing us with cheap and excellent butter. It must be remembered in comparing the prices of Danish and British products that the Danes work longer hours than we do, and in particular that there is more child labour on Danish farms. The frugality of the Danes is such that in spite of their cheap prices for the export of butter, they themselves eat twice as much margarine as butter.

CONCLUSION

There can be no doubt about the efficiency of the Danish agricultural system, nor about the responsibility of co-operation for that efficiency. Authoritative testimony is given in the following extract from the League of Nations Report on Nutrition (1937) p. 165: " The shift in the basis of Danish agriculture would scarcely have been possible had it not been for the high spirit of co-operation among the farmers of that country." And goes on to say: " It is thanks to these societies that it has been possible gradually to eliminate diseased cattle, to select the breeds and animals with the highest yield, to improve feeding stuffs, etc. In a general way, their activities, often closely combined with those of the stock-breeding co-operative societies, have been and still are decisive for all technical progress of dairy production."

Foreign observers generally are enthusiastic about the Danish co-operative system.

" Denmark, during the last half century, has been through the throes of a wonderful regeneration. Her peasantry has been emancipated from a condition of veritable serfdom; her education has been liberalized; her land system, agriculture and finance have been reorganised and brought to a pitch of excellence which is the envy of many a greater, less perfectly developed, state." [1]

[1] *Denmark and the Danes*, Harvey and Rupien, Foreword.

" The Danish peasant is the best informed in the world. More and more class distinction is disappearing among them. They have lost the suspicious reserve of the usual peasant class. And not only among the peasants but among the working class there is not that chasm between the educated and the uneducated that is found among the other countries of the world." [1]

Even Sir John Russell, with all his experience and caution, writes about the results achieved by the Danish owner-co-operator system as " prodigious " and " wonderful ".[2]

As regards the direct financial advantage to the farmer of sales and distribution through the co-operative system, it is stated that " out of the dollar spent by the consumer for ten foods in the United States in 1934, 38·5 cents went to the farmer and 61·5 cents went to the distributors and processors. As compared with this, it appears from the *Danish Statistical Yearbook* (1934) that the consumer's dollar of the Danes in 1933 was distributed 63·4 cents to the farmer and 36·6 cents to the distributors and processors." [3]

Again, the farmer is relieved from all the worry and risk of marketing, and is sure that whatever he buys from his society, be it seeds or foodstuffs or implements, it is the best obtainable at the lowest rate compatible with good quality; he is, therefore, free to devote himself altogether to the actual business of farming.

The co-operative system has another important result: there are no rich men supported by Danish farming. Apart from an insignificant number of large farms,[4] there is probably nobody among the million people supported by Danish farming who gets an income of over £1,000 a year, and probably only a few dozen who get over £500 a year—the managers of the leading co-operatives and other organisations. The owner-co-operator system, as developed in Denmark, is probably the most equalitarian system in the world. Success depends upon individual

[1] *Educational Review*, December, 1914.
[2] *Co-operation in Danish Agriculture*, Faber.
[3] *Denmark : The Co-operative Way*, by F. C. Howe, p. 73.
[4] In a census taken in 1930 there were 214 farmers with an income of over £1,000, and another 840 with between £500 and £1,000.

ability and effort; the very best men may rise to £1,000 a year; a good, though hard, life is available to the small peasant owning only five acres. There is no exploitation; there are no rich men and no very poor men; there is very little class distinction.

Is it too much to say that the Danish peasants have invented a new system of agriculture which is better than the old one from the point of view both of technical efficiency, of economic efficiency, and of social justice?

INDUSTRY

While it is true that the most remarkable feature of Danish life has been the agricultural revolution, yet industry has also grown vigorously. So much so, that nearly 30 per cent. of the working population are to-day employed in productive industry, as against just over 30 per cent. in agriculture.

As Danish agriculture in its rapid development required a constantly increasing supply of new and more scientific machinery, Danish industrialists rose to the occasion and developed many new designs. Practically the whole of the machinery required in the dairies and the bacon factories is now supplied by Danish engineers, and a good export trade has been built up in this machinery.

Danish industries have also arisen to supply the usual home needs in clothing, textiles, furniture, and for the building trade, up to the level required by the small population. What is more surprising, in view of the absence of coal, water power, and iron, is that a flourishing engineering and shipbuilding industry has grown up. This is rendered possible by the fact that freights for coal and iron from the north of England and Scotland are hardly any higher to Denmark than they are to London. Such an industry depends entirely on the brains and energy, the inventive and organising power, and initiative of the people, just as did the establishment of the cotton trade in Lancashire. Let us hope it may not prove to be equally precarious in the long run.

Some idea of the development of Danish industry in

E

the last twenty years may be obtained from the following table :—

	1914	1935
Number of establishments . . .	82,494	102,032
Total employees	350,194	462,361
Of which workmen	227,458	317,395
Works with mechanical power . .	15,579	43,414
Horse-power of machinery . . .	229,843	651,138

The same qualities have also built up a substantial shipping trade; the national fleet is well over one million tons, and earns about ten million pounds a year in gross freights, two-thirds of which is earned in purely foreign traffic, the remainder in traffic between foreign and Danish ports.

It is striking evidence of Danish efficiency that a small country with a narrowly limited domestic market, and deficient supplies of capital and raw materials, has succeeded in building up an industrial organisation which provides work for almost a third of its population at a good standard of living, and exports substantial quantities of manufactured goods.

POLITICS

The Danish constitution has been fully democratic since 1915. It is very similar to that of Sweden; there is a constitutional king, two houses of Parliament elected by adult suffrage, including women, on the basis of proportional representation. The constitution is flexible; Parliament has full powers; the King, the aristocracy, and the plutocracy have probably less power, both in theory and in fact, than in almost any other similar democracy.[1]

There are four main parties, corresponding roughly to those in Sweden. Broadly speaking, the Conservatives were in power until 1900, though during the last twenty years of this period the Farmers' influence was considerable. From 1900 to 1920 the Farmers had the chief power;

[1] Proposals are now being considered to introduce the referendum and even something approaching to single chamber government.

after 1920 the Social Democrats had increasing power. In 1929 a coalition Government was formed of Social Democrats and Radicals under Prime Minister Stauning, which is still in office. The Socialists [1] have about 45 per cent. of the members in each house, the Radicals about 9 per cent.; so that the coalition has a working majority in both houses.

It is an interesting fact that whereas the Socialists in Sweden have made a coalition with the Farmers against the Liberals and Conservatives, in Denmark the coalition is with the Radicals, the opposition consisting of Farmers and Conservatives. The reasons for this seem to be, firstly, that the Liberals in Denmark are more radical than those in Sweden; they are strongly pacifist and free-trade. Secondly, and more important, while most of the Swedish farm products are sold in Sweden, so that it has been possible for the Government in prosperous times to guarantee prices satisfactory to the farmers, in Denmark the great bulk of the agricultural products are exported at very low and competitive prices; it has, therefore, been impossible for the Government to give the farmers the same comfortable conditions which the Swedish farmers enjoy.

The task before the Danish Government has for various reasons been much more difficult than that which the Swedes have had to face. Notwithstanding this, the Government has been in power for ten years and has to a considerable extent won the confidence even of the right wing. In particular, the Prime Minister, a fine man of sixty-five, of the Viking type, with a great beard which is regarded almost as a national asset, is a man of wide experience and of considerable political capacity. He began life rolling cigars, but has educated himself and has

---

[1] The present constitution of Parliament is as follows:—

	Lower House	Upper House
Social Democrats . .	68	31
Radicals . . .	14	7
Conservatives . .	26	15
Farmers . . .	29	22
Sundry . . .	12	1
	149	76

become steadily more moderate as he has grown older. As a business man put it: " He wishes to be the grand-father of all his people ", and indeed he is fast becoming the " Grand Old Man " of Denmark.

As regards the export trade, Denmark, relying on low-priced agricultural products, has a much more difficult time than Sweden, with its timber and iron. The result is that whereas Sweden has no national debt, either at home or abroad, Denmark has a considerable external debt, to meet which she has to find two million pounds of foreign exchange every year, so that she is often in trouble for foreign exchange.

All this means a substantial burden on the budget, which, on the other hand, benefits by the fact that Denmark is still spending very little indeed on armaments.

Broadly speaking, the Government's industrial policy has been similar to that of Sweden: not to nationalise industry, but to control it in the public interest; to increase taxation on the rich so far as practicable, and to spend the income on the social services. The Government has succeeded in the seven years 1930-7 in increasing the yield of the national taxes by about 30 per cent., whereas Sweden achieved an increase of 50 per cent. in five years.

But Denmark's main trouble is industrial unemploy-ment. After all the efforts which the Socialist Govern-ment has made for ten years, after endless promises that work would be found for all, unemployment still obstinately remains at about 20 per cent. of the industrial employable workers.

And the statistics show that there is a good deal of real poverty. That an unsatisfactory class does exist is proved by a visit we paid to a low-rented municipal tenement in Copenhagen. We were taken by municipal officials, who informed us that the tenants of this block were the lowest class in any municipal building, that most of them were unemployed, and that it was difficult to collect the rents. In fact, one of the tenants who paid his own rent regularly had recently complained to them that he was in a good deal of trouble because the other tenants regarded his regularity as being bad form!

It is surprising that, in spite of all these handicaps, economists tell us that the urban standard of life is about equal to that in Sweden, and the rural standard substantially better. It is also probably true that there is less inequality of income in Denmark than in Sweden; much less, of course, than in England. Everybody one speaks to on this subject in Denmark automatically replies: "Denmark has few rich people and still fewer really poor." This is certainly the general impression among the residents, supported by the fact that Copenhagen is a very attractive and beautiful town with none of the obvious slums which in our English cities give so vivid an impression of poverty and dreariness.

The Danes are very proud of their democratic social equality, and with justice. There is a tradition of hard work; there are no rentiers; the rich business man expects his son to be a hard worker.

As in Sweden, there are only two or three secondary schools which are reserved exclusively for the children of the rich. With these exceptions, their educational system is purely democratic. There is no doubt that there is less formality and more social equality in Denmark than there is even in Sweden.

While salaries in Sweden are substantially lower than in England, in Denmark they are lower still. For instance, a university professor in England gets an average salary of perhaps £1,100 per anum; in Sweden £800, in Denmark £500. Cabinet ministers in England receive up to £5,000 per annum, in Sweden just over £1,000, in Denmark substantially less than £1,000.

In England judges in the House of Lords get a salary of £6,000 a year. In Denmark there are thirteen judges of the Supreme Court: their salary is about £650 per annum; only one of them owns a motor-car. The majority of them, as indeed of all the leaders in Danish democracy, are self-made men, who have risen from the working classes or from the peasants. It is not surprising that the outlook of the Danish judges is different from ours. One striking evidence of this is given by a custom which is growing up in the courts of inflicting fines on the basis of so many days' income of the transgressor.[1] Recently

[1] It appears that this system was first instituted in Sweden; in 1931 a statute was enacted prescribing that, as a general rule (though not for all offences), fines should be inflicted in relation to " income, fortune and economic status ". A fine is imposed in the form of so many

a rich doctor was fined £500 for a motoring accident, for which a chauffeur would probably have been fined, say, £2. This set a new standard in graduated fining; on an appeal to the Supreme Court the doctor was ultimately let off with a fine of £150, which it is said was generally approved by public opinion.

We, in England, are proud that corruption does not exist among our judges and our higher civil servants; an achievement which is commonly held to be mainly due to the relatively high salaries paid in this country. But Denmark has attained the same high standard on salaries which are out of all proportion lower; an even greater achievement, of which she has every right to be proud.

" day fines ", the day fine varying from 1–300 Kr. There have, of course, been difficulties in introducing this system in Sweden, but I understand that nobody would urge that it should be abandoned.

CHAPTER VII

DENMARK: A TRIUMPH OF EDUCATION

WHY is Denmark so efficient? Why are the inhabitants, crowded into a small country, with no natural resources except land of average quality and an average climate, so prosperous and contented?

It cannot be racial superiority; in spite of an excellent system of elementary education from 1814 they showed no signs of unusual efficiency before 1870. There can be no doubt whatever that the Danish agricultural revolution was due to the inspiration of their educational prophet, Grundtvig, who preached a rather strange mixture of Christianity, national traditions, and Liberalism, aiming at the ideal of " making good from within what has been lost from without " by means of " a simple and cheerfully active existence on earth in the service of the country ". His work led to the foundation of the famous Danish Folk High Schools, and caused a widespread spiritual revival among the farmers, which was ultimately responsible for the wonderful Danish agricultural revolution.

The process is extraordinarily interesting: the students from the High Schools went back to their villages determined to do their utmost to improve farming and life in the locality. Everywhere they took the lead in the formation of co-operative societies. As the co-operative societies got to work, they found the need for scientific advice; they began freely to use experts; they were largely responsible for the technical agricultural colleges which grew up in parallel with the co-operatives to provide the necessary experts on all different aspects of agriculture. Surely this great national achievement must be the most remarkable, indeed spectacular success ever effected by adult education.

The essential achievement of the Danish Folk High

Schools has been admirably stated by Sir Michael Sadler:—

"In the early years of the nineteenth century the Danish peasant was still unprogressive, sullen and suspicious, averse to experiment, incapable of associated enterprise. To-day he is forward-looking, cheerful, scientifically minded, resourceful, co-operative. . . . The humanities, which was all that the schools taught, did not breed ineffectuals. Between 1860 and 1880 they worked a miracle of culture in the Danish country side. The town folk were, as a whole, impervious. The peasantry was transformed. . . . It proved itself mobile, intelligent, heartily co-operative. And it is universally admitted that the agricultural population could not, but for the work of the People's High Schools, have shown adaptability so great, open-mindedness so intelligent. Grundtvig's policy had found the issue he predicted. Corporate life in an atmosphere of liberal education had given practical culture. The new leaders of the peasantry, the organisers of the new and effective co-operation, were for the most part High School men. Behind the new and swift reorganisation of one of the most conservative and individualistic industries were brains, leadership and unselfish public spirit. The People's High Schools inspired their pupils with energy and idealised labour. ' We clenched our fists as we listened to the lectures and yearned to go out and set to work.' In the schools the young men learned to trust one another. In co-operative enterprise they translated that trust into terms of associated credit." [1]

Grundtvig's educational views have been so astonishingly successful in Denmark, they are so wise, and so entirely applicable to England to-day, that I attempt shortly to summarise them.[2]

[1] *The Folk High Schools of Denmark*, published by the Oxford University Press, pp. 7–10.
[2] For a fuller statement see Noelle Davies' admirable book *Education for Life*, from which the quotations in the following pages are taken.

GRUNDTVIG'S EDUCATIONAL PHILOSOPHY

Grundtvig's aim was education for life, for " a simple and cheerfully active existence on earth ". " All around him he saw schools—schools for the Classics and for scholarship, schools for ' the three Rs ', caste schools, professional schools—but nowhere could he find a school for *life*. Yet without such a school, which would work for no mere specialist or sectional end, but for the development and enriching of the life of the whole people, he could see no hope of national regeneration." Grundtvig always envisaged education under a two-fold aspect, corresponding to the two-fold nature of man as an individual and as a member of the social organism. " His education must make him feel himself to be consciously at one with the community, sharing in its traditions of the past, its life and action in the present, and its aspirations and responsibility for the future. Thus his daily work will acquire a new significance, when he becomes aware that it may be done for the service of his nation, and, through his nation, of humanity at large. Here, once more, Grundtvig realised that to achieve his purpose the mere imparting of knowledge was not enough; inspiration must be given as well. The essential task of the school in this respect was to create that ' *spiritual sense of a unity in multiplicity* ' without which ' even the clearest insight into the organic connection of society is dead and powerless ' ".

Grundtvig urged that most of the teaching should be done through the living word, through lecture and discussion rather than through books. The students should be helped to acquire " a living sense of the greatness of their common national heritage ".

Elementary education by its very nature cannot give a full understanding of life and its real relations. Nor can secondary education, especially of the bookish type, do much more. Grundtvig believed that a country boy and girl should after school spend some years living at home and working on the land. In his opinion " the decisive age "—the time of spiritual creation—was from eighteen to twenty-five. " The period of boyhood is not the right school time. Whoever is to have good of learning must

E 2

first have lived a while and paid heed to life in himself and in others, for only so can he learn to understand books that describe life and throw light on it."

For these purposes he had no high opinion of the university. " Would it be exaggerated to assume that three-fourths of the students of Copenhagen can hardly write Danish; know no other history than that of which they have learnt some fragments at school and at the university; have no other idea of philosophy than that it is a wretched dry thing they must learn for their second examination; know nothing else of poetry than that it is something—usually lies—which rhymes or at all events—God knows why—sounds very pretty; and, finally, have no higher goal for their students than at most to get a first class at their final examination, and after that—a well-paid job? "

" Scholarship is one thing, and education and fitness for life another; they may well be united, but not in the case of the majority; they must not be hostile to each other; they must be kept separate, otherwise they seek to drive each other out, and necessarily . . . spoil each other." Scholarship will lead scholars astray " if it is not confronted by an education of the people which obliges it to take present-day life and the moment into consideration, just as the education of the people will soon degenerate into a superficial polish if scholarship does not keep it alive ".

He came to the conclusion that the best method of giving the education he wanted would be through a new type of school, the Folk High School. The schools were to be residential, and the daily intercourse of teachers and students should play an important part in creating " the spiritual sense of a unity in multiplicity ". Grundtvig laid great stress on freedom; the whole thing was to be voluntary, and under no circumstances must there be any examinations. The aim was not " to give a certificate for the possession of knowledge, but to impel youth to waken to the realisation of its own human value, of its civic duties, and its spiritual destiny ".

Grundtvig thought that the right attitude could best be taught through history, Danish language, and song. " History, as the experience of life on a large scale, is not only the best, but the only thing by means of which one can rightly enlighten young people," he declared, and again, " Since history embraces the most noteworthy words and deeds of the human race, in which human nature reveals itself and to which all scientific progress belongs, all human knowledge is historical at bottom, and knowledge of the past is the only means of understanding the present and laying wise plans for the future."

" The type of history teaching which Grundtvig wished to prevail in the ' school for life ' was not the critical or bookish type. One of his chief complaints against the existing education system was that it over-developed the critical faculties at the expense of the other sides of human nature. ' We are all educated to be critics instead of creators,' he said. Scholarship, indeed, had gained by this; but the gain was only temporary, for eventually ' the eternal criticising will exhaust our human life-force, and give free play to the animal impulses which never die out '. Already it had inflicted such injury on the moral and spiritual life of the community that only by turning into another path could spiritual bankruptcy be avoided. To Grundtvig the growth of this critical and destructive mentality seemed to be bound up with the ' bookwormi-ness ' which he regarded as one of the great faults of his generation."

As regards the teaching of language, " ' The mother tongue has its home neither in the brain of scholars nor even in the pen of the best writers, but in *the mouth of the people*, and it is here, and not there, that the mother tongue must live and move and work, express and extend Danish patriotism, enlightenment, joy, and gladness.' The chief means of education in the mother tongue should be free lecturing and ' living conversation ', combined with a study of ' the popular, and especially the historical and poetical, part of our national literature ', and of the traditional proverbs which ' enshrine the spirit of the language '.

" Side by side with the mother tongue went song as the third great medium of living education—song, which, as Grundtvig said, lifts us above the earth and gives us a glimpse of the eternal—song, through which the individual may reach the highest point of harmony, both within himself and with his fellows. What Grundtvig wanted here was not conventional solo singing, but hearty, natural, united song, in which the words had equal value with the music."

There are to-day in existence about forty Folk High Schools based on Grundtvig's educational philosophy. These schools have still so important an effect on Danish agriculture that it seems worth while to describe shortly how they function.

THE DANISH FOLK HIGH SCHOOLS TO-DAY.

The Danish Folk High Schools are residential schools, where the pupils live as a single community with the director, his family, and the teachers. Most of them are housed in fairly good buildings, some distance from a town, as a rule the young men for a term of five months in the winter and the women three months in the summer. They are generally from twenty to twenty-five years of age.

The Danish Folk High Schools are said to be freer than those of any other country in three ways:—

1. Anybody can start his own Folk High School. If he can for two years attract the necessary pupils and teaches something like the accepted subjects, his school is recognised by the government for a grant. In ninety years 160 schools have been started, of which sixty survive to-day.

2. The director of the school can appoint his own teachers with whatever qualifications he likes and at whatever remuneration he agrees with them. As the schools are always poor, salaries are lower than in the ordinary elementary school, and teachers are only attracted by love of the work.

3. The director is free to teach any religious or political doctrine he pleases, and may influence the students as much as he can. In fact, the schools are started by those who have some doctrine to spread. About 80 per cent. of the pupils attend schools where the philosophy of Grundtvig is preached; the others are divided among different religious and political movements.

There is a government inspector, an ex-Foreign Minister, who visits all the schools to give what help he can and to see that the conditions of the grant are fulfilled, but there is no interference whatever with the full liberty of the director to teach any doctrine he may desire.

The students come almost entirely from the farming community. Ninety per cent. of them have only had an elementary-school education, after which they have had five or six years working on the land before coming to the Folk High School. There are at present about 6,000 pupils in these schools; approximately one-quarter of the whole agricultural population has attended them. The majority of them have attended no classes since leaving the elementary school; during the first few weeks they find the whole thing very difficult; after that all goes well in most cases.

FINANCE

The fee is something less than £1 a week, which is inclusive of residence, food, teaching, and everything else. A modest grant is given by the state. Salaries are very low; the director must reconcile himself to a life of simplicity, and almost of poverty. Standards are, for instance, much lower than in the hostels of an English provincial university, but the food is adequate and the health of the students good.

The Frederiksborg school has 100 men pupils for five months in the winter and 150 women for three months in the summer, each of whom pays £4 a month. There is also a government grant of £600 a year, so that the total income of the school is just about £4,000 per annum. The staff is as follows: the director and his wife, four other whole-time teachers, two university graduates, who are being trained as librarians and get no salary, and a Swedish and a Norwegian woman, who teach their respective languages and get no salary. There is also a housekeeper, with eight girls under her.

Anybody who tries to work out a detailed budget on this basis will see how very economically the whole thing is run.

Coleg Harlech was founded some years ago in Wales to be run on the lines of the Danish Folk High Schools; it is no larger than the Frederiksborg school, but the

Danish government grant of £600 per annum has to be replaced by voluntary subscriptions of £7,000 per annum to carry on Coleg Harlech successfully.

AIMS

The Danish Folk High Schools are non-vocational. They have no *practical* aim; their object is to enable their pupils to live a richer life, to understand the great problems of the day, to learn to undertake their full responsibility as citizens of a free democratic state.

" They repeat over and over again that the pupils should go back to the work they have been doing before, and that they should enter into their work with greater zest and pleasure and with a clearer understanding of the value of the work for themselves and for others."

The Folk High School movement is, though not perhaps so powerful as it was fifty or sixty years ago, still of great importance; in fact, it is generally regarded to-day as being essential to the effective carrying on of the Danish agricultural co-operative movement.

It is often said that the great days of the Folk High Schools were in the 80's and 90's, and that they give to-day no similar leadership in patriotism or love of the land or joy in fostering growth. Many farmers feel that their fate is controlled by great impersonal forces, such as violent fluctuations in world prices or sudden reductions in the available market in England owing to circumstances entirely beyond their control. The farmers often feel that the Government does not understand their needs, many of the ablest young farmers gravitate to the city where earnings are much higher, and on the other hand, inferior people, who find a difficulty in making a living in the city, tend to gravitate to the country. This movement, which exists to some extent in all partly industrialised countries, is a grave danger to the efficiency of agriculture.

Although it is probably true that the Folk High Schools are not the power they were in their early days, there can be no doubt that they are still one of the strongest means of inducing the peasants to resist the attractions of the town, and to appreciate the importance and the pleasures of agricultural life.

CONCLUSION

The result of this humanistic adult education has been the evolution of an agricultural system which is a model for the whole world. Up to about 1870 there was no co-operation. Danish agriculture was individualistic, unprogressive, and not specially efficient, even though there had been a good system of elementary education from 1814, and a strong tradition of peasant independence. Now the Danes are the most highly educated, co-operative, friendly, and cultured race of farmers in the world.

And the success of co-operative farming has had a very important secondary effect; the average farmer is a member of several small co-operatives, he votes for the committee of management and watches their work year by year. He knows them well enough to choose them on their practical qualities; he would never think of selecting a tub-thumper or a demagogue, and his experience in this way must be helpful in electing sensible political leaders.

Then again, the system is an excellent training for the members of the boards of the co-operatives, who get actual experience of democratic work. Almost every man of brains, energy, and character has the opportunity of practical experience in running a democratic organisation. The best of them will be elected to the national co-operatives, and will get experience of business on a large scale, including export business, and will thus be in contact not only with national but with world affairs.

Thus the very elaborate and extensive Danish co-operative system, which is in itself the result of the educational work of Grundtvig, is in its turn one of the most effective examples of education for democracy through experience.

The whole story of the Danish agricultural revolution is a wonderful illustration of the effects of the right kind of education, education with one central aim : to send out the students into the world " with clenched fists "— enthusiastically determined to do everything in their power, along with their fellows, to strengthen the farming and the common life of Denmark.

This moral drive led to the whole co-operative system, which in its turn has resulted, on the one hand in the spread of the agricultural college and the production of the most scientific peasants in the world, and on the other hand in the almost complete ownership of the land by the farmers who work it.

And so this magnificent agricultural system is due to three things: education, co-operation, ownership. And the greatest of these is education, for the whole structure rests ultimately on the faith in science, and the religion of co-operation and democracy, with which the Folk High Schools have inspired the Danish farmer.

CHAPTER VIII

NORWAY

I visited Norway after Sweden and Denmark; in many ways the three countries are remarkably similar. In this chapter I accordingly attempt to deal only with certain points in Norway which tend to throw fresh light on Scandinavian politics.

Norway has an immense area, sparsely populated by just under three million people; it is very mountainous, and its chief natural wealth is in great forests and rivers and waterfalls. It is the richest country in Europe in potential hydro-electric power, of which about two million horse-power have already been developed.

Norway is, geographically, even further removed than Sweden from the turmoil of European politics; like Sweden, it has no substantial minorities, either racial or religious.

Fifty years ago the great bulk of the population were engaged in agriculture and fishing; to-day just under 30 per cent. are directly engaged in productive agriculture, and so rapid has the recent development of industry been that it employs almost the same number.

Norway is one of the oldest kingdoms of Europe, constituted as such before the end of the ninth century. Towards the end of the fourteenth century it was united with Denmark, but remained by name and by right a separate kingdom. After the Napoleonic Wars Norway separated from Denmark and was united with Sweden. The union lasted until 1905, but became increasingly difficult. In particular, as the shipping trade developed, Norway began to demand a separate consular service, which Sweden was not willing to give. Norway never liked the union with her more powerful neighbour, which had twice her population, was richer, and inclined to be more conservative. Finally, after a period of increasing tension, the union was peacefully broken by mutual consent in 1905—evidence that the democratic spirit of compromise was already strong in both countries. To-day old differences are forgotten, and the relations between the two countries are excellent.

The present Foreign Minister, Herr Koht, Professor of History at the University of Oslo, in his book *The Rise of the Peasants* stresses one thing as exceedingly important to Norwegian democracy: that throughout recorded history the peasants in Norway have never been serfs. In spite of all attempts and despite great poverty at times, the Norwegian peasant has always had a considerable degree of freedom and independence.

As in the other Scandinavian countries, a good deal has been done in the last fifty years to split up the large estates; there are to-day over 250,000 farms, 94 per cent. of which are owned by those who work them. The great majority of these farms are, of course, small; 90 per cent. have less than twenty-five acres of farm land, though many of them have forest land in addition, from which they get fuel and timber for sale.

Industrial developments in Norway have been to a great extent based on timber, and, as in Sweden, a substantial export trade has been built up in the various timber products. The standard of life is generally held to be comparable with that in Sweden; though, as in that country, there is real poverty among the fisher folk and forest workers.

Norway's one great city is Oslo, with about a quarter of a million inhabitants.[1] It is a very pleasant town to live in, well laid out, situated in beautiful surroundings amidst fiords and wooded hills. A really fine new town hall has just been completed on a splendid waterfront site.

A Sea-faring People

Norway is the land of fiords; measuring along the shores of the fiords the coast line stretches for 12,000 miles: one-half the distance round the world at the equator. And quite naturally the outstanding feature of Norwegian life is their

[1] Including the suburbs, the population is about 400,000.

sea-faring habit. More than any other European people, the Norwegians have been a race of sailors from the days of the Vikings, not only fighting and fishing, but also trading by sea: the records show that a thousand years ago the Norwegians had an export trade in dried cod fish.

The coast is rich in fishing grounds, especially in the north. The Norwegian fisherman is usually his own master, owner or part owner of craft and tackle. There are many small co-operative groups, each member contributing to the cost of boat and tackle, and the profits being divided according to the amount contributed. There are over 100,000 fishermen and a fleet of more than 30,000 vessels. In the hard school of these northern waters the crews are trained which man the Norwegian whaling and merchant fleets.

Norway was the pioneer in whaling in the Antarctic and is still the leading whaling nation. The life of the seaman on the whaling ships is hard and difficult, and it is an interesting fact that British whalers are manned mainly by Norwegian sailors and officers.

The Norwegian merchant marine consists of about 2,000 ships, passenger, freight, and whaling vessels, with a total tonnage of nearly 5,000,000. Though Norway is so small a country, it has the fourth largest national fleet in the world, only Great Britain, the United States, and Japan having a larger tonnage. In proportion to the population, Norway is by far the world's greatest shipping nation. Shipping plays an exceedingly important part in the Norwegian national economy. The net income from shipping, that is, the salaries, wages, overheads, and profits, which come into the country each year, has in normal years recently amounted to about £10,000,000; in the boom year 1937 it rose to £25,000,000. In average years this net income amounts to no less than 10 per cent. of the total national income, and must therefore have an important effect on the standard of living.

This great shipping trade has been due to the enterprise of Norwegians; on the one hand, the officers and sailors, on the other, the business men who plan and control the work. The fleet is, of course, far larger than is necessary to deal with the Norwegian imports and exports. In many cases the Norwegian ship trades on a regular route, perhaps in the Far East; it stays out there year after year, and a steady stream of money comes home to Norway in the form of wages and profits. It is a remarkable example of national initiative and business ability.

It must be noted that the Norwegian merchant marine competes with the merchant ships of other nations, nearly all of which have received or are receiving subsidies from their governments. In Norway shipping is so important and other industrial undertakings so relatively small, that the Government has never given any subsidy to shipping, and indeed it is said to be unthinkable that they should ever be able to afford to do so. On the contrary, shipping has to contribute heavily through taxation to the general national welfare.

The Labour Government appreciates the importance of the shipping industry to Norwegian life, and has apparently no idea of attempting to nationalise it. On the other hand, it is naturally anxious to secure the best possible conditions for the sailors, and there has been a good deal of pressure to enforce the eight-hour day. Shipowners take the view that standards of wages and conditions are good in Norwegian ships, indeed probably better than they are in any other country, and that to make them *much* better than those of the other great competing nations, for instance by enforcing an eight-hour day while other nations are still working longer hours, would be very dangerous, and might even destroy the industry.

One intelligent and successful shipowner whom I met was rather hoping for an immediate depression in the shipping industry, lest the Government should act on the assumption that good conditions were likely to persist indefinitely, and on that mistaken assumption should impose taxes or social conditions which might sap the resources of the industry in the next slump.

POLITICS

The Parliament, known as the Storting, consists of 150 members, elected for a term of three years [1] by proportional representation; it cannot be dissolved before the end of the

---

[1] Now extended to four years.

three years' period. For some purposes the chamber splits itself into two separate houses, but essentially it is single chamber government with remarkably few checks and balances. All men and women have the right to vote at the age of twenty-three.

The ministers need not necessarily be members of Parliament; they do not vote, but have the right to attend and speak whenever they wish to do so.

As in Sweden, the house is split up into a number of standing committees, to which all important matters are referred. All permanent committees of the Storting are elected on the principle of proportional representation, and every single member acts on one of the committees. It is the custom for each member of a committee to be made responsible for some definite portion of a bill. He has to report on it to the committee and, if necessary, to deal with it in the house. A private member therefore has definite constructive responsibility, of a kind which rarely falls to the lot of a private member in the British House. It is generally agreed that this has a very valuable educative effect on the members. Similar conditions prevail in the Swedish and Danish Parliaments, and perhaps go some way to account for the high degree of constructive competence and of power of compromise shown by the Labour ministers to-day in all three Scandinavian Parliaments.

The Prime Minister was a labourer in Norway and a lumberjack in Canada. One of the opposition leaders said that he had worked closely with him for fifteen years; though formerly extreme, he was now most practical. He trusted him absolutely: " Never once has he failed to carry out in public what he promised me in private."

A leading business man said: " It is really astounding to see how the Prime Minister is trusted by all parties."

There are several highly competent persons in the Cabinet. The Government as a whole is powerful, effective, and moderate, and is so regarded by nearly all groups in Norway.

EXTREME SOCIALISM?

Almost everybody told me that the Labour party in Norway was distinguished from that in Sweden and

Denmark by being more extreme. There is no doubt whatever that during the last thirty years this has been true. From 1905, the date of Norwegian independence, the development of industry has been exceedingly rapid. There was only a small foundation of old and experienced industrial workers; large numbers of young men from the farms, with a strong national tradition of peasant independence going back many hundred years, were suddenly thrust into the totally new conditions of industry. It was almost a case of " humanity uprooted ". Everything was new. It is perhaps not unnatural that they joined the Labour party, and in pre-war days took up syndicalism with a good deal of vigour. After the war, following the fashion of the times, there was a strong Marxist movement, and for three or four years until 1923 the majority Socialist party was actually a member of the Communist International.

Gradually, as they acquired experience of industrial conditions, the Labour party became more moderate. In 1928 the first Labour minority Government was formed, but the middle classes were still afraid of them, and ejected them after only three weeks in office, because some of the banks were being seriously weakened by a flight of capital from Norway. So far as I have been able to trace, this is the only case in the three Scandinavian countries where a Socialist Government has caused such fear among capitalists that they have begun sending their capital abroad on any scale that was dangerous to the financial stability of the country.

The following table shows the position of the various parties after the last four elections:—

	1927	1930	1933	1936
Labour [1]	59	47	69	70 (46%)
Communist	2	0	0	0
Conservative	—	42	31	36
Farmers	—	25	23	18
Liberal	—	34	25	23
Sundry	—	2	2	3
	—	150	150	150

[1] The Norwegian Socialists have not yet accepted the title of Social

In 1930, the Labour party, for the last time up to the present, fought the election on a rather extreme programme, which united the middle-class parties against them, and were heavily defeated as a result. From 61 members they fell to 47 : a very big reduction for one election under proportional representation, affording evidence in support of the view that the Scandinavian electorates during the last ten years have been against extreme parties and programmes.

In 1933 the Labour party in their election campaign declared explicitly in favour of democracy, and on a more moderate programme they got 69 members out of 150; but it was not until 1935 that the other parties handed over the government to them. Since then, the present Labour party have been in power; in the 1936 election they gained one seat. They have not formed a coalition with any of the other parties, but carry on with the support of the Farmers, or sometimes of the Liberals.

The Labour party, including the Government, still regard themselves as ideologically more radical than the other Scandinavian governments, but admit that in practice they behave much as the others do. They have learnt the need for moderation and for democracy; in practice, their aim is freedom, social equality, and no exploitation; nobody ever mentioned Karl Marx to me. All the Socialists I spoke to wanted to discuss what were the next practical steps that could be taken for the welfare of the people as a whole.

A leader of the Farmers party gave me the following opinion : " The Socialists had a narrow view till they got into power : to buy farm produce at the lowest cost, regardless of the standard of living of the peasants. This was also the policy of the Liberal Government; but in 1935 the Socialists came to an agreement with the farmers to ' level up ' agricultural prices. It was on this account that the Farmers supported the Socialists in forming a government. The policy since then has been a Socialist agricultural policy : to try to ensure that the farmer gets a fair price for his produce, giving a reasonable standard of

---

Democrats, as has been done in Sweden and Denmark. " Labour party " is perhaps the best English name.

living for the peasant; also that the worker shall have good wages, so that each group shall have effective purchasing power to strengthen the other group. Although there is no coalition with the Farmers, they work together on much the same lines as in Sweden."

He still regarded the Socialists with some suspicion as unstable and potentially dangerous, but he thought that if they had another three years at the head of a minority government, the added experience would make it safe to trust them not to abuse the full powers of a majority government.

Co-operation between Farmers and Labour in Norway is not on such close and friendly terms as in Sweden. Hence the need for the present Government to seek alternating support, from the Farmers for its economic policies, from the Liberals for educational reforms and development of the social services.

It should be added that in practice the Norwegian Labour party have pursued a policy almost identical with that of the Swedes: increasing taxation (their taxes are the heaviest of the three Scandinavian countries), improving social services, controlling capitalism and exploitation in any ways they could discover which would not damage the initiative and success of business. The only things I could discover which the Norwegians have done which are more socialistic than what has been done in Sweden are that they have prohibited all Sunday papers for the benefit of the workers in the newspaper industry,[1] and that nearly all the cinemas in Norway have been municipalised, with great profit to the municipalities and, it is said, with a tendency to improve the quality of the films shown. It is typically Scandinavian that both these things were done long before the Labour party formed their first government.

The Labour party were, as in Sweden, fortunate in the date when they took office. There were 165,000 unemployed; times improved rapidly, 1937 was a boom year, especially in shipping, and unemployment has now fallen to 100,000; they have not been as successful as in Sweden in securing full employment.

Strikes have been more serious in Norway than in the other countries; there were several big conflicts between

---

[1] This was done by trade-union action.

1921 and 1931. Since the Labour Government took office strikes have been less. The Government and their press have endeavoured to avoid strikes instead of taking an active part on the side of the workers as they invariably do when in opposition.

CONCLUSION

The two outstanding points that strike one about recent Norwegian history are, first, the success of shipping, due to the natural qualities of the sailors and the initiative of the entrepreneurs; and second, the fact that the Labour party were twenty years ago extreme and revolutionary; since then they have become steadily more moderate, and, as in the case of the other Scandinavian countries, when they were entrusted with the powers of government they at once adopted a practical and constructive policy; they have ceased talking about Marxism; they do their best to avoid strikes. In short, although they are still said to be more radical than the other Governments, the Norwegian Labour party are showing the same highly encouraging power to form a realistic, progressive, and successful Government, working steadily, one step at a time, towards a just and democratic social order.

But it is probable that the political situation in Norway is less stable than in Sweden and Denmark. A Norwegian authority sums up as follows: " One factor ought to be kept in mind. Owing to the radical, half-Communist half-syndicalist past of the majority of trade unionists in the older unions, there is a good deal of opposition among the rank and file against the moderate policies pursued by the present leadership of the unions and the party. It is impossible, therefore, to say with certainty whether the present policy will be maintained or not if the economic situation changes radically. We do not even know for certain whether the efforts which are being made at the moment on the part of the Trade Union Centre to secure prolongation of existing agreements without a stoppage will succeed. They are meeting with considerable opposition on the part of industrial workers who feel that they have not got their rightful share of the improvement in the economic situation since 1935.

"I think it is safe to say that the present orientation of Labour is less stable in Norway than it is in Denmark and Sweden."

CHAPTER IX

FINLAND: A DEMOCRACY IN THE MAKING

FINLAND offers an instructive example of the growth of democracy under great difficulties and in a much earlier stage than the Scandinavian countries.

Geographically, Finland has considerable similarities to Norway and Sweden. It is a large country, its area being considerably greater than that of Great Britain and Ireland, sparsely populated by only 3·8 million people. It has immense areas of forests, the greatest in Europe outside Russia, and large reserves of water power. The climate is like that of the Scandinavian countries; and the peasants have a similar strong tradition of independence.

There the resemblance ends. Historically, the Scandinavian countries, remote from the clash of European wars and independent of foreign control, have had the opportunity of steadily developing their democracies through long years of peace and security. Finland, after being united with Sweden for 600 years, was invaded by Russia in 1808 and after a bitterly fought war was incorporated in the Russian Empire as a Grand Duchy with its own constitution and the Russian Emperor as its constitutional monarch. During the 19th century there was a gradual growth of Finnish national sentiment and culture; up to the end of that century the internal government of the country was dominated by the Swedish Finlanders. The Swedish Finlanders numbered only about 10 per cent. of the population, but as a result of the long union with Sweden included a large governing class, which occupied most of the leading positions both as regards wealth and power.

The collapse of the Russian campaign against Japan, and the revolutionary risings in Russia gave an opportunity for a strong move towards independence in Finland. In 1906 Finland succeeded, as a consequence of one of the few really *general* strikes in history, in securing a very democratic constitution: a single Parliament elected by proportional representation by the vote of every citizen, rich or poor, man or woman, on equal terms. It was actually the first grant of woman suffrage in Europe. Suddenly the Finnish Diet became perhaps the most democratic Parliament in the world; and in the ensuing elections the Social Democrats secured 40 per cent. of the votes, which was at that time also a world record.

But the Czar quickly reasserted his authority, and refused to allow the Diet to use the powers given to it by the constitution. However, he did not force the Finns to serve in the Great War, and in spite of political difficulties, industry developed rapidly.

In 1917, as the result of the Russian revolution, the Diet declared Finland an independent country. There was almost immediately a Red *coup d'état* declaring a Socialist workers' republic. The middle classes organised, being known as Whites, and a civil war ensued in which the Reds were helped by Russia and the Whites by Germany, ending in complete victory for the Whites.

This civil war is now officially known as the war of independence. According to Mr. J. Hampden Jackson, there is " wildly conflicting evidence as to what really happened ".[1] In his opinion, the two sides fought for independence as they saw it: " It stands out as a civil war of Finns against Finns, the old Finland of yeomen and pastors against the new proletariat of the towns helped by the landless peasants. It was fought with the terrible brutality which is peculiar to class conflicts. . . . These atrocities, committed by a race which has proved itself to be one of the most humane and law-abiding in the world, can scarcely be imagined by anyone who thinks of them by the calm light of peace-time."

Fortunately, the civil war lasted only a few months; a new Diet was elected; the Social Democrats pledged themselves to constitutional action and expelled the Communists, who formed a separate party. The com-

[1] *Finland*, p. 101.

position of the Diet as elected, and later Diets, is given in the following table.

PARTIES IN THE DIET

	Swedes	Tories	Liberals	Farmers	Social Democrats	Communists	Fascists
1907	25	58	26	9	80	—	—
1919	22	28	26	42	80	—	—
1922	25	35	15	45	53	27	—
1929	23	28	7	60	59	23	—
1930	21	42	11	59	66	—	—
1933	21	32	11	53	78	—	14
1936	21	34	7	53	83	—	14

The Diet adopted the constitution of 1905 with considerable modifications, giving a good deal of power to the President. The middle-class parties governed till 1930, with one short-lived Socialist government in 1927, though (except for one brief period) the Socialists were always the largest single party. Industry continued to develop rapidly, and all went fairly well till the serious slump of 1929.

Meantime fear of Russia and of Communism among the middle classes had never abated. The White organisation had been continued as a Civic Guard, which had always regarded the Communist party as dangerous revolutionaries. In 1930 there was an outbreak of Fascist activity; Communists were attacked. Some of them were beaten and thrown over the wire into Russia, and, as feeling developed, some Social Democrats, and even the popular Liberal ex-President, were kidnapped.

The Government gave way to the storm and took active measures. They passed an act forbidding the entry into Parliament of the members of any party working for the overthrow of the state, disbanded the Communist party and imprisoned Communist leaders. Things then settled down under a rather right-wing government, and industrial conditions rapidly improved.

Political feeling also improved, and after the 1936 election the first stable left-wing Government was formed by a coalition of the Socialists, Agriculturalists, and Liberals.

The Cabinet consisted of a Liberal Prime Minister, another Liberal, five Socialists, and five Agriculturalists. This Government is in office to-day. The strong man of the Cabinet is the Socialist leader, Tanner, an experienced and moderate politician. The Government seems to display the typical Scandinavian qualities of practical common sense and moderation.

AGRICULTURE

From time immemorial the people of Finland had owned land. There were only a few very large estates, but a considerable number of small ones, mostly worked by the farmer-owners and their families. With the growth in population during the 18th and early 19th centuries, many strips of forest land had been leased for cultivation in return for labour and a certain amount of produce. At the coming of the Industrial Revolution, which greatly increased the value of timber and therefore of forest land, the whole social balance of Finland was upset. The landlords refused to give new leases and tightened up the old ones, so that the tenants were often forced to surrender them, with the result that a new landless class was created, most of the former tenant-farmers having to become labourers, many others migrating to the towns to obtain work in the new mills.

After the founding of the Republic, one of the most urgent tasks before the Government of Finland was to enable the existing tenant-farmers and cottagers to acquire their own holdings, and to provide new holdings for the landless. In 1918 state loans were provided to enable peasants to purchase the land they were working, the price to be based on the value in 1914. Although there was an outcry from the landlords that this level was too low, on the whole they were willing to come to terms.

Little was done regarding the second part of the problem till 1922, when the Agrarian party leader formed a ministry, with the support of the Social Democrats and Progressives, pledging himself to find land for the landless. It was a difficult task to face, but in 1927 a law was passed providing state aid for the purchase of two types of holding, small farms and cottage–allotment plots respectively, from the larger estates, the land so purchased to have been previously uncultivated.

This policy was an unqualified success in three respects: firstly, it increased the number of peasant proprietors, many leaseholders becoming owners, and many of the formerly landless class becoming cottage and allotment owners. There are to-day 285,000 separate farms, the great bulk of them owned by those who work them; of these 216,000 have an area of less than twenty-five acres. Altogether, in spite of the large amount of industrial development that has taken place, no less than 60 per cent. of the population of Finland gains its livelihood to-day principally by agriculture. Secondly, the area under cultivation was considerably enlarged, and thirdly, the productivity of the land was greatly increased.

The state has not been primarily responsible for the great progress that has been made, although it has undertaken research work and provided loans. The main responsibility lies with the farmers, in their thoroughness and in their collaboration through the co-operative movement, which began in 1901, and has steadily grown, until to-day more than half the adult population are members. A considerable number of co-operative dairies have been established, also many other agricultural producers' co-operatives, with the result that a new export trade in agricultural products is growing up. In the period 1911–15 to 1937 the total volume of agricultural production has been multiplied by three.[1] Even so, it has by no means yet reached the intensity or the yields of Denmark or the other Scandinavian countries.[2]

INDUSTRY

Industry in Finland has always been mainly based on her possession of immense forests. In the second half of the 19th century, the Industrial Revolution began to penetrate into Finland; the possibilities of using her water power for industrial purposes were realised, and a

---

[1] *Unitas—Nordiska Bank Review,* November 1938, p. 97.
[2] *Ibid.,* p. 96.

new process for pulping wood was developed, as also were the means of communication. A commercial treaty was made with Russia, and a tariff, advantageous to Finland, was agreed. There was a steady movement towards free trade and exports became freely available.

Steadily, year by year, the wood industry grew, new branches were developed, and the volume of exports increased, the country becoming more and more prosperous and wealthy. Then came the Great War, offering unlimited opportunities to Finland of exporting war materials and equipment to Russia. Prices soared, but wages did not increase proportionately, and a large amount of cheap Russian labour was sent over to help in the production of the necessary goods.

After the war, and with the independence of Finland, her trade with Russia came to an abrupt end and she was forced to find new markets and develop new export trade, which was done with marked success. New machinery was installed and electric power was applied to the wood industry, with the result that the volume of trade again increased, prices keeping at their high level. The effects of this boom were felt by all classes; the exporters made large profits and extended their plant, many agricultural workers found winter employment in timber camps, and their increased purchasing power created a demand for new industries for manufactured goods for home consumption. There was also great expansion in the building trade, as most of the towns were rebuilt during this period.

During the years 1929–32 the world slump was felt in Finland and trade rapidly declined, causing a serious unemployment problem, to meet which the Government adopted a policy of public works and took measures to check the fall in agricultural prices by increasing duties on imported cereals, pork, and eggs. By 1932 the worst was over, and from then on conditions quickly improved, until by 1937 the volume and value of exports had reached their previous prosperity peak of 1928. Unfortunately, the brunt of the depression fell on the workers, whose wages were lower than ever, and even now, although wages have risen again and unemployment has been practically abolished, the old rates of pay have not been restored.

Money wages to-day in Finland are about half the level of those in Sweden.[1]

Good profits have been made and there has been money available for capital development, new industries being developed and the old ones remodelled. Strikes have been infrequent in recent years. As a result of efficient management, on the one hand, and of low wages, on the other, the output of industry has increased by about 150 per cent. in the last fifteen years,[2] and net exports have increased by no less than 250 per cent. in the last twenty years.[3]

This rapid increase in the export trade has not been accompanied by a corresponding increase in imports, and the favourable trade balance resulting has enabled Finland to convert two-thirds of her foreign debt into internal debt during the last ten years;[4] and, as the more patriotic Finns do not fail to remind one, Finland is the only country which is paying in full its (very small) debt to the United States.

Since the recovery in 1932, trade conditions have been quite different from those of the pre-slump years. There has been a great improvement in trade relations with Great Britain, which now takes the greater part of Finnish exports. Although wood and its products still account for 83 per cent. of the total exports, instead of the bulk of this being in the form of raw materials as was previously the case, there has been a large increase in the proportion of manufactured goods: pulp, cardboard and paper, cellulose, etc.

To sum up, there is no strong trade-union movement, partly due to the fact that industrial development on a large scale is comparatively recent, and partly to the fact that the trade unions were dissolved during the Fascist regime in 1930. Although they have grown again and now have a membership of about 90,000, they are still relatively weak; collective bargaining has not yet been achieved in the most important industries.

[1] Bank of Finland Monthly Bulletin, September 1937.
[2] Unitas—Nordiska Bank Review, November 1938, p. 105.
[3] Ibid., p. 108.
[4] Ibid., p. 144.

F

STANDARD OF LIVING

I have already pointed out that wages in Finland are about half those prevailing in Sweden. On the other hand, prices are low, too, so that although the wage level is low the standard of living is comparatively high. As in the Scandinavian countries, the range of incomes is much less than in England; in 1931 there were only twelve people in Finland with incomes exceeding £6,500 per annum.

In spite of the growth of industrialism, the town workers still comprise only a small proportion of the working-class population, less than 20 per cent. being town dwellers in 1935. Living in a town in Finland, however, is vastly different from living in a typical industrial city in England. There are no slums, because there are no old towns; there is no dirt, because of the universal use of electricity in industry. The only really large town is Helsingfors, with a population of rather more than a quarter of a million. It is a pleasant and attractive city, very like the Scandinavian capitals, situated on a promontory surrounded by water, and with plenty of undulating forest land stretching away to the north for future development. Town planning has been practised from the beginning; suitable outside areas have been scheduled by the council for the building of summer cabins for the workers. There is a certain amount of overcrowding; no subsidies have as yet been given for the housing of large poor families. On the whole rents are high, as in the Scandinavian countries.

Finland is definitely behind the Scandinavian countries in the social services. For instance, there is no unemployment insurance; and although the matter has been discussed, it has as yet received little support. A system of old-age and disablement pensions has now been introduced, which is to come into operation in 1940, and there is a fairly good system of poor relief. The greatest social problem, however, is public health, to which a good deal of money and energy is being devoted.

In contrast with the weakness of the trade unions, consumers' co-operation is strong and effective throughout the country, although, owing to a split in the movement between urban and rural societies, development has been somewhat restricted, and has not been so successful as in Sweden.

Nevertheless, a good deal has been achieved in the way of setting price levels of certain articles.

The conditions provided by the consumers' co-operatives in Helsingfors are good. They have a forty-seven hour week, and holidays with pay; and they claim that they have improved conditions of workers in shops, have raised the quality of the shops themselves, and have kept down prices. The larger of the two local co-operatives has a fair-sized island, only a hundred yards from the mainland, which is kept for the recreation of its 2,400 employees.

It is interesting to compare Finland and Sweden from an industrial and economic point of view. In both countries industry has developed at a surprising speed in recent years. Sweden is fully trade-unionised and its success is built up on collective bargaining. In Finland the trade unions are still weak; wages and the standard of life are much lower than in Sweden, but industrial expansion has been similar. Both of them have for the last two years reached boom conditions with very little unemployment, but by very different routes.

CULTURE

The Finns have developed their culture to a high level in spite of centuries of invasion and conquest. Sweden brought them under the influence of western civilisation. For centuries they have been a comparatively literate people; to-day less than 1 per cent. of the adult population is illiterate. The public libraries are of a very high standard, and Helsingfors boasts the largest bookshop in Europe in spite of its comparatively small population. To quote Mr. Hampden Jackson: "Whereas in England there are hardly a dozen decent bookshops outside the university towns, in Finland there is a bookshop in every large village, even within the Arctic Circle. And the equipment of the public libraries is something to make eyes used to the gloomy and impoverished institutions of most English country towns open wide in wonder. As for the press, there were no less than 209 daily papers in circulation in 1936 (of which 23 were in the Swedish language) and 557 reviews. Circulation figures are not available, but 219,500,000 copies of registered journals and periodicals were distributed through the post alone in 1936; in other words, 59 copies for every man, woman, and child of the population." [1]

As regards education, this has been developed rapidly and one-seventh of the annual state expenditure is to-day devoted to it. Less emphasis is laid on purely academic education and more on vocational and physical training than in England. There is a compulsory system of elementary education from the age of seven to thirteen, after which the children go to advanced schools for two years for vocational courses. It is actually reported [2] that 40 per cent. of the children go on to secondary schools, and the proportion of students at the universities is remarkably high. There are also many trade schools for boys and girls, technical, commercial, industrial, agricultural, which give instruction in all branches of industry, in forestry, in dairy farming, and so on. A few Folk High Schools, modelled on the Danish Folk High Schools, also exist.

Architecture is a most flourishing art, Finland having produced several architects of international reputation during the present century. Music is also well developed, the country having many noted musicians, headed, of course, by Sibelius. Literature is good, but unfortunately it cannot be translated effectively owing to its peculiar Finnish quality. The dramatic art has developed rapidly and holds a noteworthy position in the cultural life of the nation. There are said to be a thousand theatres run by the city, trade unions, co-operative societies, etc., often with a single professional. As a whole, the theatre is largely a medium not only of amusement, but also of education and culture.

Conclusion

Finland to-day offers an exceedingly interesting study of democracy steadily developing under considerable difficulties. The civil war was fought only twenty years ago. The Fascist rising, with its kidnappings and beatings, occurred less than ten years ago. There has only been a very short time in which to soften the undemocratic men-

---

[1] *Finland*, p. 216–17. [2] *Ibid.*, p. 220.

tality of regarding one's opponents with hatred as Reds or Whites.

Even to-day, Communists are still in prison. According to the right, those in prison are men who have been proved before the courts to be guilty of treason to the state, who have plotted to upset the regime by force. According to the left, they include men who were ejected from Russia after having worked there, and who are otherwise perfectly innocent.

In November 1938 the coalition Government declared that the Nazi party, which includes fourteen members of the Diet, came under the Act which was passed in 1930 to suppress parties who were working against the interest of the state. The majority of the Diet held that the party intended the overthrow of the democratic state by violence, and that it was much too dangerous to allow such dogmas to be preached. Only forty out of 200 members of the Diet voted against the suppression. But the law courts held that the vote was out of order, so that the matter is at the time of writing in suspense. This action on the part of the Government shows, on the one hand, their desire to preserve democracy even by drastic steps; on the other, their lack of confidence in the inherent strength of Finnish democracy to resist subversive propaganda by ordinary means.

The Finnish Civil Guard has still 200,000 members. A young doctor I met proudly showed me his card as colonel of a battalion, and said " We saved the country from Russia in 1917. The Civil Guard is still essential to protect Finland from Russia and from Communism, which are for us the same thing."

There are about 200,000 Finns in Carelia, which is in Russia. There is a Carelia irredenta movement among the more extreme sections of Finnish youth, in spite of the fact that Russia has a population fifty times as large as that of Finland. As an illustration of the power of nationalist feeling, a university lecturer told me of one of his students who had been to the border and looked at Carelia through the barbed wire; she felt so deeply that she burst into tears in telling him about it.

There is a good deal of feeling about the position of the Swedish Finlanders, who dominated Finland up to the end of the nineteenth century. The Swedish Finlanders constitute about 10 per cent. of the population, and include rich and powerful industrialists on the one hand, and peasants and fishermen on the other. There is a feeling among many sections of the Finns that the Swedes abused their power in the past, and that it is high time now that they should cease to be a separate group causing disunity and weakness, and should become an integral part of a strong and united nation. A strong objection, therefore, is taken to the use of the Swedish language: while I was in Helsingfors a resolution was passed by a society, including almost the whole of the Finnish students at Helsingfors University, demanding that Swedish be no longer recognised as an official language.

No legislation has been passed discriminating against the Swedish Finlanders, but they feel that they are no longer being given their fair share of recognition and of positions. The question is fairly acute; the Swedish Finlanders are certainly not being treated with anything approaching the tolerance of the minorities in Switzerland.

All this shows what strong feelings persist from the days of violence. But there is another side to the picture. Mr. Hampden Jackson states: "Of all the neighbours of Soviet Russia there is none that enjoys so high a degree of political liberty as Finland."[1] The coalition of Social Democrats and Agriculturalists contains members who actually fought on opposite sides in the civil war, yet the two parties have been co-operating in a friendly and democratic fashion both in Parliament and as members of the Government for the last two years. This must be regarded as a very remarkable achievement. Experienced public men of different parties with whom I discussed the matter were of opinion that Finland was firmly set on the path of democracy, and that if she could be left alone for the next ten years, secure both from foreign aggression and from too much foreign propaganda, it could be regarded as a reasonable certainty that old hatreds would be more and more forgotten, and that Finland would steadily work towards a really progressive and tolerant democracy.

[1] *Finland*, p. 17.

CHAPTER X

SCANDINAVIAN ACHIEVEMENT

I HAVE shown in the chapters on Switzerland and Finland such conclusions as I have come to about the working of democracy in those countries. On the other hand, Denmark, Norway and Sweden are so alike in many respects that it seems worth while to try to summarise their remarkable achievements as a whole.

The populations are small and homogeneous; there are no substantial minorities, either racial or religious; they have had a long period of peace and security in which to develop democratic institutions.

AGRICULTURE

They have all large peasant populations, a strong tradition of peasant independence, and have done much in the last fifty years to split up large estates and to encourage peasant ownership. Sweden has approximately 250,000 peasant owners, Norway 235,000, and Denmark 200,000, and each country has a highly developed and efficient system of agricultural co-operation. This system of small owner-co-operators, most fully developed in Denmark, is approved by all three Social Democratic Governments. It provides a working alternative to Socialism, and its success is no doubt one of the reasons why extreme theoretical Socialism is so weak in Scandinavia.

INDUSTRY

All three have developed industry vigorously during the last fifty years and have now an approximately equal balance between their industrial and agricultural populations. Sweden has built up an important export trade in high-class industrial products, based on her timber, iron, and water power; Norway has developed the largest shipping industry in the world in proportion to population; Denmark, though possessing no raw materials, has succeeded in developing an efficient industry with a substantial export trade.

POLITICS

All have flexible democratic constitutions, with adult suffrage for men and women, and proportional representation. There are no politically privileged classes, Parliament has supreme power.

All have the same four main political parties: Socialist, Conservative, Farmer, and Liberal: none of them has any other parties of importance. In all three there has been a steady increase in the Social Democratic vote, which is to-day in all cases about double the size of the next largest party. In Denmark and Norway the Socialists have about 45 per cent. of the total vote; in Sweden, at the last election, just over 50 per cent.

LABOUR GOVERNMENTS

In Denmark there has been a Social Democratic Goverment for ten years in coalition with the Liberals. In Sweden there has been a Social Democratic Government for six years with the support of the Farmers; during the last two years there has been an actual coalition between the two parties. In Norway the Social Democrats have governed for three and a half years as a minority government supported sometimes by the Farmers, sometimes by the Liberals.

All three Social Democratic parties were pretty left-wing twenty years ago—the Norwegian party belonged to the Communist International till 1923. All three have become steadily more moderate and practical. They have abandoned, at least for a time, their socialism in the sense of nationalisation, for which they have not been able to get a majority, and have concentrated instead on practical measures for the benefit of the common man—on the " socialisation of consumption ". They are endeavouring to abolish poverty and unemployment, to raise the standard of living, to check monopoly, exploitation, and abuse; for such programmes they have had no difficulty in securing a steady majority.

LEADERSHIP

The Socialist leadership in all three countries can fairly be described as outstandingly good. All three Prime Ministers were manual workers and have educated themselves to a high standard; all three have the qualities enumerated by Gladstone when praising Lord Aberdeen: calmness, solidity, judgment, knowledge of the subject, and moderation of view. They live in modest circumstances; none of them has an income of over £1,000 a year, no official house, no motor-car; it is even said that none of them has a really competent private secretary. The Prime Minister of Sweden goes to his office in a tram; the Norwegian ministers, seeing off the Crown Prince recently, walked to the station on a rainy afternoon.

One never hears any of the leaders accused of the kind of social ambition or vanity which was so disastrous to the Labour Government in England.

All three Cabinets have men of high quality; all include not only men who were manual workers, but university graduates and in some cases professors. The Cabinets have somehow achieved a striking democratic ability for effective action without arousing violent opposition.

ACHIEVEMENT UNDER THE SOCIALIST GOVERNMENTS

Agriculture. In all three countries the Socialist parties have endeavoured to act as a workers' and peasants' government and to hold a fair balance between town and country. The problem of adjusting agricultural prices and industrial wages for this purpose has been tackled with outstanding success by the Swedish Government, where the problem has been easier owing to the general prosperity and to the fact that there is little export of agricultural produce. Denmark has had the greatest difficulty, owing to the fact that the bulk of the agricultural produce is exported.

F 2

Industry. In all three countries the relations between capital and labour are good; strikes have decreased since the Socialist Government came into power. All the Governments have increased the taxation on industry, but not to the extent of interfering with enterprise, nor of causing any serious bad feeling.

Finance. Production has improved and direct taxation has been increased; the tax yield has, therefore, increased rapidly, and the social services have been greatly developed in all three countries. The national credit of Sweden and Norway is excellent; that of Denmark not so good, as she has neither the valuable exports of Sweden nor shipping on the Norwegian scale. Sweden has gone further towards the abolition of unemployment than any other democracy.

Social Life. Their practical arts, especially architecture, are of a high standard. Their cities are beautiful, healthy, and well-planned, excellent places to live in. Their society is democratic in the sense that there is much real social equality. This is no doubt largely due to the fact that, being small countries, there are relatively few rich men.

The difference between the income of the manual worker, on the one hand, and of the well-paid professional classes on the other, is much smaller than in England, as shown by the table on page 171. This table is based on the salary of the street sweeper in municipal employment, which seems to be a convenient unit. It will be seen that the salary of a judge of the Supreme Court in England is equal to that of thirty-five British street sweepers; in Sweden and Switzerland the judge is reckoned as worth rather less than six street sweepers, and in Denmark as being worth not more than four! There are similar differences in the salaries of other leading professional men. The whole range in England is of the order of 35–1; in the other countries of the order of 6 or 7–1.

Standard of Living. All three countries are poor in natural resources, but all three have achieved a good standard of living. It is exceedingly difficult to get any reliable figures on this matter. I have read what is available in English, and have discussed the question for hours with leading economists in all three countries. All of them refused to provide any figures, on the ground that the whole subject was too complicated and difficult to deal with statistically,

The following table is intended to show the whole-time average earnings of various representative persons in England, Denmark, Sweden, and Switzerland, with the object of finding out what is the range between the rich and the poor in each country. As the unit, I have taken the male street sweeper, working for a large municipality, Manchester, Copenhagen, Stockholm, Bern. The idea is to take this as the unit, and to compare the others proportionately.

The salaries are expressed in pounds sterling to make comparison easy. All figures refer to 1938.

	England		Denmark		Sweden		Switzerland	
	Salary	Proportion	Salary	Proportion	Salary	Proportion	Salary	Proportion
	£		£		£		£	
Street sweeper	145	1	150	1	210	1	223	1
Highest salary paid by municipality	3,500	24	1,000	6·5	1,300	6	631	3
Teacher in elementary school, average length of service	300	2	240	1·5	384	2	354	1·5
Professor, average length of service	1,100	7·5	500	3	735	3·5	620	3
Judge of Supreme Court	5,000	35	600	4	1,147	5·5	1,214	5·5
Head civil servant	3,000	20	600	4	1,044	5	728	3
Member of Cabinet	5,000	35	900	6	1,300	6	1,600	7

though one of them hopes to have worked out a scientific method of comparison in the course of the next ten years! The nearest I got to anything definite was a letter from the International Labour Office in which they state: " Real wages in the three Scandinavian countries are slightly higher than those in Great Britain, which again appear to be a little higher than those in Switzerland." [1]

My own conclusion is that the standard of living of the workers, both urban and rural, is in all three countries certainly as good as in England, and in many ways probably better. There is less unemployment and really serious poverty at the bottom, and on the other hand they have not the very rich section represented by the City and West End of London and the large country houses of England.

Efficiency

The most common attack on democracy nowadays is to talk of its inefficiency, to condemn it as aimless, leaderless, and incompetent. What evidence do our democracies provide on this matter?

In the first place, there is one thing that all dictatorships and democracies aim at: a good standard of living for the people. I have shown how difficult it is to arrive at an accurate measure of the standard of living of the whole of the people, but few economists would doubt that the following grouping as to the standards of living of the most prosperous countries in the world to-day is substantially correct.

Group I: The United States, Canada, Australia, New Zealand.

Group II: Norway, Sweden, Denmark, Switzerland, England, Holland.

Group III: includes Finland, Germany, Italy.

---

[1] The full statement by the I.L.O. is as follows:—

" Although the International Labour Office have never attempted to make comparisons of standards of living between different countries, partly because some of the important elements in such a comparison are almost entirely lacking, they have from time to time made some rough comparisons of real wages which, since they have not taken account of certain elements, cannot be said to give more

The British-speaking democracies in Group I have certain special advantages and ought perhaps in fairness to be eliminated in making comparisons with dictatorships. Group II includes four of the democracies we are studying. Not a single dictatorship has succeeded in reaching this standard; though it would be difficult to suggest that our four democracies have any natural advantages over Germany and Italy. Is it not a fair conclusion that the peaceful small democracies have, in fact, been efficient enough to achieve a better standard of living than any dictatorship in the world?

There are, of course, certain things which democracies do not tackle efficiently. One is preparation for war. Dictatorships, who believe in war, are naturally more efficient, or at least begin preparations for war earlier than any democracy is likely to do.

A much more serious case is unemployment. The abolition of unemployment presents tremendous difficulties to a capitalist democracy; Socialists argue with some reason that this failure is due to the profit motive, and that a socialist democracy would be able to deal with the problem without undue difficulty. In my view this is perhaps the weakest spot in democracy nowadays, and I think it not unlikely that a considerable degree of socialism may be necessary in order to enable governments to keep the whole of the people constantly employed. Unemployment both in Norway and Denmark is still at a relatively high level among industrial trade-unionists. But the efforts of Sweden to abolish unemployment in a capitalist democracy, which has only a very moderate amount of socialised industry, are distinctly encouraging. Nobody could deny that the present Swedish Government is tackling this problem with energy and efficiency.

Finally, in considering the efficiency of democracy, one must admit that a dictator, able to impose a certain object on the whole of the people, can often succeed in working

than an approximate indication of relative purchasing power, in terms of food prices, of individual real wages." The International Labour Office (so its London office tells me) would not go further than this general statement that apparently "real wages in the three Scandinavian countries are slightly higher than those in Great Britain, which again appear to be a little higher than those in Switzerland; all the differences, however, appear to be small."

towards that object more efficiently than any democracy can hope to do, since owing to variety of human nature the democracies in peace time rarely or never work for a single object, except in the very broad sense of working for a social order in which every individual shall be able to enjoy freedom and happiness. But there are values in democracy: freedom and justice and kindliness and truth, which for the democrat are, or should be, infinitely higher than efficiency. Democrats believe that democracy in its broadest sense, that is to say, government based on the will of the people, is the only type of government through which these values can ever be reached. That I believe, generally speaking, to be the faith of the citizens of the five democracies which we have been studying.

Conclusion

Finally, it will be agreed that the post-war record of the three Scandinavian countries is most encouraging. They have faced their problems with skill and courage, with common sense and tolerance, in a truly democratic spirit. They have shown that it is possible to combine full and free discussion with effective leadership; they have shown unity as regards external affairs, combined with efficiency and steady progress in home affairs.

Among the mass of people the habit of discussion is widespread; in all cases the press is sensible and moderate. The common man values his freedom and independence, and at the same time believes that other people have the right to exist as well as himself, and has some capacity for seeing other points of view. He has the qualities demanded by the Chinese philosopher Lin Yutang, who says: " An educated man should, above all, be a reasonable being, who is always characterised by his common sense, his love of moderation and restraint, and his hatred of abstract theories and logical extremes."

It has been said that democracy is discussion: in this sense all three countries are definitely democratic. And in all three the people have learnt how to elect good leaders: rarely does one find a cabinet minister of the demagogue or tub-thumper type. Leadership, both in politics and elsewhere, is conspicuous for its integrity, its moderation and tolerance, and at the same time for its activity and competence.

These small democracies are the most encouraging thing in the world to-day. They prove that men are learning to overcome the complexities of the machine age, to make use for the benefit of mankind of the inventions of science. Most important of all, the Scandinavian countries are the only countries in Europe which, since the war, whilst elsewhere the newer democracies have been destroyed and the older ones are on the defensive, have become steadily more democratic, steadily more prosperous and more contented. They have passed what is often thought to be the critical stage in democratic development: that is to say, their governments no longer represent the privileged classes; all three of them have for some years been governed by representatives of the poorer half of the population.

The three Socialist governments are now firmly established, they have shown moderation and good sense; but nobody doubts their determination gradually to build up a just social order with equality of opportunity for all, political, economic, educational, and social. The richer classes are fighting a delaying action, but there is no bad feeling, no flight of money to foreign countries; nobody suggests the prospect of violent resistance from the right at any stage. On the contrary, the governments are given credit for their achievement and are steadily gaining votes; it may be regarded almost as a certainty that, given peace, these three countries will gradually build up a free, friendly, and efficient democratic order, governed by the mass of the people, in which every individual will more and more be given the opportunity of living in peace and security a full and satisfactory life.

The three Scandinavian countries are to-day disturbed and frightened by the threat of aggression from the south. The whole-hearted devotion of their governments to the improvement of conditions of life has already been interrupted by the need for rearmament. The freedom of the press is being hampered under foreign threats; everybody is uneasy and uncertain. It will be a tragedy of world-wide importance if the peaceful development of the Scandinavian democracies is prevented by external aggression.

CHAPTER XI

WHAT IS A DEMOCRACY?

I BEGAN this book by asking a number of questions about democracy. At least partial answers have been given to most of them in the preceding chapters; in Chapter X I have summed up my answers as to how far the small democracies have been successful and efficient. I must now try to answer two more difficult questions: What are the distinguishing characteristics of the citizens of these democracies? What values do they believe in? And secondly, what political institutions have they developed?

There is inevitably a close relation between the character of the citizens and their political institutions which must react on one another.

One thing in particular seems to be typical of all democracies:

THE SMALL SELF-GOVERNING GROUP

It is often held that the foundation of democracy is local self-government. For instance, Lord Bryce writes as follows:

" The best school of democracy, and the best guarantee for its success, is the practice of local self-government. . . . Local institutions train men not only to work for others but also to work effectively with others. They develop common sense, reasonableness, judgment, sociability. Those who have to bring their minds together learn the need for concession and compromise. A man has the opportunity of showing what is in him, and commending himself to his fellow-citizens. Two useful habits are formed, that of recognising the worth of knowledge and tact in public affairs, and that of judging men by performance rather than by professions or promises." [1]

I have shown that this is undoubtedly true of the small commune in Switzerland and of the agricultural co-operative society in Denmark. Self-government in a relatively small group, where the problems are familiar and simple and where it is clear that unless the individual citizen himself undertakes the necessary daily work it will not be done, does undeniably give certain qualities which are fundamental to democracy, and which perhaps cannot be developed at all except in such small groups. I have dealt with the development of these qualities through local self-government pretty fully in the chapter on Switzerland, and through co-operation in the chapter on Denmark, and have shown in both cases how group experience has developed independence, tolerance, the habit of public service and of working with others, and practical common sense.

In all five countries there is a tradition of active local government, and co-operation has in recent years been spreading fast in all of them. There are also trade-union branches, which give effective training for citizenship, perhaps most conspicuously in Sweden. There are also other groups of various kinds; but in these countries local government, co-operatives, and trade-union branches undoubtedly provide the great bulk of the education which the citizens receive through the practice of co-operating with one another in small groups.

As I have shown in the cases of Zurich and Stockholm local government when it comes to large cities is much less effective in preparation for democratic citizenship. In Zurich a good deal is apparently achieved by means of the referendum and by the strong Swiss tradition of local responsibility. In Stockholm I doubt whether local government is playing any important part in preparing its citizens for democracy.

Our five small democracies are fortunate in having relatively few great industrial cities. I fear that in England, where the majority of people live in large cities, local government is to-day doing very little to train them for democracy.

[1] *Modern Democracies*, p. 149.

This may well prove to be a grave danger to the stability of democracy in this country.

Lord Bryce was too sweeping when he suggested that local self-government was always a good school of democracy. It all depends on size: in great cities local self-government has little value in training the mass of the citizens for democracy, but in smaller communities, such as the five democracies we are studying, where there are strong traditions of self-government, where the unit is small and the problems simple and intelligible to the ordinary citizen, there is little doubt that Lord Bryce's statement is true. To put it more generally, it is probably right to say that an essential ingredient of a satisfactory democracy is that a considerable proportion of the people should have experience of active participation in the work of small self-governing groups, whether in connection with local government, trade unions, co-operatives or other forms of activity.

THE CITIZEN

Coming now to the question of the character of the individual citizen, I suggest that the following conclusions can fairly be drawn.

Peace. The mass of the people in all these countries are firm lovers of peace. Internally, they are peaceful and friendly with one another, strikes are getting fewer; even in the newest of the democracies, Finland, the hatreds of the civil war are rapidly being replaced by friendly tolerance. Externally, it is no doubt true to say that owing to their small size they are forced to adopt a peaceful attitude: but nobody who knows them doubts that all these countries are genuine lovers of peace. Denmark has gone further than any other country in the world in disarming. Norway and Sweden have distinguished themselves by their peaceful separation into two kingdoms in 1906, and by the foundation of the Nobel Peace Prize.

Freedom. They are independent peoples, loving and insisting on freedom. Discussion of political matters is widespread, the citizens are free to speak their minds frankly, to criticise and oppose the government. It is true that there have been certain limitations on the freedom of the press in recent months, but this is a reluctant concession to the danger of external aggression.

Belief in freedom may be regarded as the basis of a related group of qualities, of which the second is

Tolerance. Democrats respect one another's opinions and are tolerant of different views. The outstanding example is the friendly goodwill which prevails between men of different race, language, and religion in Switzerland. History shows that as democracy develops it builds traditions of tolerance which, as General Smuts says, " is the very essence of our civilisation ".

Truth. Perhaps the most fundamental difference between the democrat and the dictator lies in their respective attitude to public discussion of political matters. In a dictatorship the common man is expected to accept the " truth " on the guidance of his leader, who claims to know it by natural wisdom or by intuition. Criticism or discussion of the dictator's " truth " is the greatest crime a man can commit. In democracy the truth must be sought for by the methods of science, by full and free discussion, by " the drudgery of hard thinking ". Under a dictatorship criticism leads to the concentration camp; under democracy constructive criticism is the greatest service a citizen can render. The treatment of the Trotsky opposition in Russia, and of Röhm and his friends in Germany, is in startling contrast with the respect paid to the opposition leaders in these small democracies.

Justice. Freedom, tolerance and truth are only possible in a community where the rule of law prevails, where equal justice for all, regardless of race, class, or creed, is a fundamental principle. Needless to say, this is the case within practical limits in all our five democracies.

Kindliness. There is evidence in all these countries that kindliness has grown with the prevalence of peace and security. They are conspicuously friendly nations. The outstanding humanitarian statesman of the century was the Norwegian, Fridtjof Nansen.

Public Service. There is in all these countries an active and widespread public opinion, which does not confine itself to thought but includes the necessary action. There are sufficient citizens who feel their responsibilities strongly enough to see that the government is carried on in the general good, and that private interests are not allowed undue power. There are plenty of competent citizens

willing to face the trouble and expense of election both for
national and local government. There is very little
corruption.

Co-operative Habit. They have the co-operative habit of
working with and for others. The finest examples of this
which I came across were the village of Blatten in Switzerland and the co-operative societies in Denmark. They
have practical common sense and the qualities of the good
committee man.

Equality. The people demand equality of political rights
and have pretty well achieved it. There is also a steady
approach to social equality; the Prime Ministers live in
modest houses and use the tram like anybody else; even
the kings in the Scandinavian countries lead simple lives.
Economic equality has by no means been achieved, but,
as would be expected where the mass of the people control
the government, they are more and more demanding a
steady approach towards economic equality. The range
of professional incomes is only about a fifth in these countries
of what it is in England; taxation on the rich, and especially
on unearned incomes, is gradually being increased; the
new device of basing fines, not on so many pounds, but on
so many days' income, is further evidence of the steady
approach towards economic equality.

DEMOCRATIC INSTITUTIONS

What institutions have these various countries devised in
order to enable them to live in accordance with their
democratic outlook?

In political terms, democratic values are expressed by the
democratic method of government: the method of taking
political decisions, not by imposing the will of a dictator or
of a group on the public, but by seeking to arrive at the
greatest possible measure of common agreement. Bassett
has given the best description of this aspect of democracy
as a method of government: [1] that all matters of controversy should be fully and publicly discussed, that every
effort should be made to seek agreement by compromise,
that the majority has the duty of considering the views of the

[1] *The Essentials of Parliamentary Democracy.*

minority in legislating, and that the minority has the duty, having had such consideration, to accept and work any new laws in a friendly spirit. The essence of democratic government is the search for agreement, and the effort to avoid coercion.

This summarises very well the methods of government in force in our five democracies. Our next problem is, therefore, to consider the political institutions through which these methods are carried out.

The institutions in the different countries show great similarity. They all have parliamentary government based on adult suffrage of men and women, with the one rather surprising exception that women in Switzerland have no votes. Parliament is supreme in all countries in the sense that there are no checks and balances of the type of the House of Lords or the powers of the American President or Supreme Court. Though there are written constitutions, they can easily be changed by Parliament; though there are kings in the Scandinavian countries who have certain theoretical powers, they are not regarded as being an obstacle to the carrying out of the will of the people.

In Sweden the Upper House is elected indirectly and the elections are for a rather long period, so that there is an element of delay in making Parliament as a whole correspond to any swing in opinion. In Norway democracy is perhaps most complete; Parliament is elected for four years and has practically full power to do what it likes. Denmark is now considering a constitution similar to that of Norway.

But the people are not always satisfied by the fact that Parliament is in full control of national affairs. There is in some cases a suspicion that Parliament itself, even though elected for limited periods and by proportional representation, may not always represent the true will of the people. Hence the demand for the referendum. This has been in force for many years in Switzerland, both locally and nationally, and on the whole people are strongly in favour of it. Parliament, on the other hand, feels that in many cases it is essential to act quickly, and that in these instances the referendum is undesirable; the Swiss Parliament is to-day struggling to maintain its independent power of action by passing measures under emergency clauses, which enables it to avoid the referendum. But on the whole the tendency among the people seems to be towards the referendum: Denmark is at present discussing its introduction, and on rare occasions it has been tried in the other countries.

It is undoubtedly true that there is a conscious effort in all these countries to mould their institutions in such a way as to make the will of the majority of the people effective, and that they have already all gone a long way in that direction.

CONCLUSION

Let me now endeavour to sum up shortly the answers which have emerged to our questions as to what are the characteristics of democratic citizens and democratic institutions.

1. The small self-governing group, whether in its traditional form of local government or in its newer form of trade-union or co-operative branches, is an important, perhaps indeed a vital, method of preparation for the responsibilities of democratic citizenship.

2. The citizens of all our five democracies share three groups of qualities:

The freedom group—they are lovers of peace and freedom, of justice and truth; they are tolerant and kindly.

The service group—they have a sense of public responsibility and the habit of friendly co-operation in the public service.

The equality group—there is a strong demand for political equality, and an increasing demand for social and economic equality.

3. *Institutions.* All five countries have a free and varied press, and full opportunities of free speech and of public meeting; that is to say, opportunities for the formation of an informed public opinion.

They all have freely elected governing bodies, both local and national, which they have made as responsive as possible to public opinion. The citizens maintain a jealous watch on the working both of the civil service and of their elected representatives.

CHAPTER XII

WHY HAVE THESE DEMOCRACIES
SUCCEEDED?

I MUST try now to answer the last, the most important, and by far the most difficult of my original questions. Why have these five small countries developed so successfully and on such democratic lines? I only wish it were possible to give a definite answer to this question, so that we could all learn and copy their methods. Unfortunately, the whole thing is far too complicated and difficult for such simple solutions. But I think some points emerge pretty clearly.

In the first place, it seems certain that the democratic way of living must be a gradual growth, and it is pretty clear that it depends on two things: peace, and economic security. All these countries have had a long record of peaceful development, and for the last fifty years on the whole a steadily rising standard of economic wellbeing. It is probable that under these conditions human beings will always tend to develop the democratic qualities of tolerance and friendly co-operation. The importance of economic wellbeing to democracy is dramatically illustrated by the collapse of the Nazi movement among the Swedish farmers when fair prices were guaranteed to them in 1932. The most surprising instance of rapid growth of democratic feeling is the recent history of Finland, which is developing a really democratic spirit within twenty years of a civil war.

Another advantage which all these countries have is that their populations are small. I have pointed out over and over again in the previous chapters the comparative ease of managing a small population as against the difficult world-wide problems of a country like Great Britain.

Two other factors of historic importance are the tradition

of peasant independence and of local government, which have prevailed to a considerable extent in all these countries for hundreds of years. The peasants have never been serfs; there has been a strong tradition of local government and a good deal of parliamentary independence at most periods of history. There has never been a really powerful centralised bureaucracy such as France and Germany have experienced. Peace and security and a tradition of local independence have certainly contributed much to laying the foundations of Scandinavian democracy.

Climate may be important. Northerners are slow and thoughtful as compared with the lively and excitable Mediterranean nations. Whether or not there are inherited qualities in the Scandinavians which make for democracy, or whether their good sense is due entirely to environment, we cannot tell.

We can, therefore, I think say with some confidence that there are four important reasons for the success of our five democracies:—

1. Their small size.
2. A long period of peace.
3. Economic security and wellbeing.
4. The cool climate of the north probably helps towards the practical common sense which is so important for democratic citizenship.

LEADERSHIP

We may assume then that these four causes are largely responsible for the democratic characteristics of the citizens of these northern countries which I discussed in the last chapter. But there is one aspect of successful democracy which I have not yet discussed, and which is perhaps the most important of all: the power of the people to select good representatives, to create conditions under which these representatives will develop into competent statesmen; and then, what is no less important, the people having selected a good government must be willing to allow it to govern. The government must be supported by an active and intelligent public opinion, which will welcome leadership and will help the government in overriding that great danger to democracy—the power of well-organised and wealthy sectional interests.

Leadership is just as important in a democracy as in a dictatorship, and one of the dangers of incompetent democrats is the belief that leadership can be dispensed with, and that the people can actually govern themselves. One of the most untrue and dangerous statements ever made by a leading democrat was President Jackson's: "The duties of all public offices are or at least admit of being made so plain and simple that men of intelligence may readily qualify themselves for their performance."

In Switzerland the leadership in local government seems to be good; for instance, the president of Blatten and the president of Zurich have both held office for many years and through their personalities have effective powers of leadership. But there is a widespread suspicion of powerful leaders in Switzerland, and many people think that Swisss national politics suffer from the lack of outstanding leaders. The President is appointed for a single year and is a person of no importance. Many educated Swiss do not even know his name. This seems to be a real weakness in Swiss democracy.

The position is different in the Scandinavian countries. I did not have an opportunity of studying their local government, except in Stockholm, where it was frankly rather disappointing. But from what I was told, leadership in Scandinavian local government generally is honest and competent.

But perhaps the most striking and most important thing about Scandinavian democracy is, as I have already shown, the outstanding ability of the national governments. The country in which I studied this most carefully was Sweden, and I think that it is no exaggeration to say that the reputation which Sweden has in the world to-day for successful democracy is mainly due to the altogether really admirable leadership of their present Socialist Government. In view of this, I spent some considerable time in trying to find out why the members of the Swedish Cabinet are so exceptionally good.

There are two reasons which may account for the selection of competent persons as representatives. Firstly, as I have explained, in the case of a small village like Blatten oratory counts for little, efficient achievement for much, in the selection of leaders. The larger the electoral unit, the more difficult it is for the elector to judge between the different candidates, and the more likely it is that the mere orator will get undue preference. The small size of the Scandinavian democracies is undoubtedly a factor in the selection of good leaders.

Secondly, although the salaries that can be reached through the civil service and through politics are limited to about £1,000 a year, yet the ambitious Socialist can probably do at least as well from the financial point of view in public life as he can in other vocations.

There are in Sweden two normal avenues to political preferment for Socialists: firstly, through the trade unions, as in this country, and secondly, through journalism. There are about thirty-two Socialist newspapers: it is easy for a young man to earn a living on them. At the present time no less than twenty-six Socialist editors are members of Parliament. This opportunity of promotion for young Socialists hardly exists in England.

Turning now to the question of the training for leadership which is received by a member of Parliament in Sweden, there are at least four reasons why this training seems likely to be better than it is in England.

1. The work of the Riksdag is conducted to a very large extent by committees which have actual constructive work to do. These committees are an excellent training ground for statesmanship. From my experience in the House of Commons and from what I have been able to learn of the Riksdag, my opinion is that the latter does train its members for practical constructive work, whereas in the House of Commons the member spends an exceedingly small proportion of his time on constructive committee work. On the whole, I believe that the House of Commons' training tends to emphasise party spirit and successful debating rather than constructive work.

For instance, I shall never forget one of my early experiences when I was elected to Parliament in 1923. The first Labour Government was in office, and one of the earliest things it did was to bring in a private member's omnibus bill, which included one very urgent clause for the prevention of the unfair eviction of tenants. There were clauses which the Conservatives intensely disliked (and I think with some justice); they, therefore, obstructed the work of the committee with great skill and persistence; so much so that after sitting for no less than twenty days there were still seventeen amendments to be dealt with before the first word of the first clause of the bill! This seemed to me, as a young and ardent reformer just elected to Parliament, a shocking state of affairs. But what worried me most was that nobody seemed to mind—the Conservatives were pleased; the Labour members said it could not be helped because they expected to do the same when the Conservatives got into power. I should add that the leaders of the Conservatives on this committee were Mr. Neville Chamberlain and Sir Kingsley Wood! I believe that obstruction of this sort would not be tolerated in the Swedish Parliament, and indeed that no party would think of attempting it.

2. The system of proportional representation, leading to minority governments, means that no party can have entirely its own way. There must be constant compromise on all the measures that are introduced. It would be impossible to govern at all if each party tried to insist on its own "principles". I have always been rather strongly against proportional representation, on the ground that the British two-party system was the best way of producing a strong government and good leadership. And undoubtedly the wrong kind of proportional representation, such as that which prevailed in Germany after the war, with an almost unlimited number of small parties, could hardly be expected to work well in any country. But nobody can deny that proportional representation in the three Scandinavian countries during the last ten years has worked at least as well as, and probably indeed better than, any other system of election has worked in any democracy. Nobody in any of the five democracies which we are studying in this book seems to have any hesitation in supporting the present system of proportional representation. Certainly in Sweden at the present time it is showing itself consistent both with full and free democratic discussion and with effective leadership.

3. The traditions of the civil service in these countries are important. One frequently finds what is to us a rather

surprising combination of civil servant and politician in one individual. The outstanding case of this is the Swiss executive committee, which runs right through the Swiss political system from the smallest commune to the federal executive, and which consists of leading politicians who are appointed as salaried members of the whole-time executive committee. They are very like members of our Cabinet, and carry out administrative duties while still remaining members of their political parties.

In the Scandinavian countries civil servants are often members of Parliament; this keeps the civil servant in closer contact with current affairs, and prevents the academic attitude which tends to prevail in Whitehall; on the other hand, the civil servant, when he becomes a politician, accustomed as he is to constructive work, tends to reduce the factious party spirit in political life. There may be drawbacks to the civil servant-politician; there is no doubt whatever that the system has important advantages.

4. The Swedish educational system seems to be better and more practical than ours if judged by its effect on leading politicians and professors. The most striking example of this is in the field of economics. The Swedish economists were the first to work out the new financial methods of dealing with unemployment, and as theoretical economists are known throughout the world. But they are not content to be merely theoretical; at least four of them are not only outstanding economists, but also experienced members of Parliament in close touch with practical affairs.

On the other hand, the members of the Cabinet who are particularly concerned with economic questions thoroughly understand economic theory. In fact, I have been told that Mr. Wigforss, Minister of Finance, understands it at least as well as any professor, and somehow manages to combine this academic excellence with outstanding qualities as a practical statesman. And his chief civil servant is not a man of academic and classical training secluded in Whitehall, but a highly trained economist in constant touch with practical affairs.

It would have been quite impossible for the Socialist Government to carry through their very successful experiments in the reduction of unemployment without this high degree of economic education among the leading statesmen and civil servants. Sweden provides the strongest possible evidence of the vital importance of properly educated leaders in the complex affairs of a modern democratic society. Swedish statesmen and civil servants understand the theoretical basis of their practical actions; Swedish professors are interested in and understand the practical applications of their theories. The Swedes seem largely to have overcome the modern curse of narrow specialisation: their statesmen are professors and their professors statesmen.

EDUCATION FOR CITIZENSHIP

But education is important not only for the leaders but for the whole mass of the people. The importance of the right sort of education has never been put more forcibly than by Plato: "We call man a gentle animal; and, if nature has been kind to him and his education has been right, he is the most gentle and god-like of creatures. But if his education is inadequate or bad, he becomes the most savage of all the products of the earth."

The education to which Plato refers may be the education of experience, which is certainly the most important factor in the small Swiss village. But formal education in schools is always important; as the area of government grows larger and the problems become more remote and more difficult to understand, so does formal education become more important.

All five countries have good systems of compulsory elementary education which have been in existence much longer than in England. In Sweden it has recently been decided that modern history should be taught as far as possible in the elementary schools, and that these courses shall be known, not as "History" but as "History and Civics". None of these countries has anything resembling our dual system—one set of schools for the well-to-do governing class and another for the rank and file. Their whole educational system, elementary and secondary, is on a non-class basis. This is generally considered important, especially perhaps in Switzerland, in discouraging class consciousness and in fostering a democratic way of life.

All these countries have compulsory continued education for about four years after the elementary school, and I think it is true to say that in all cases citizenship is a compulsory subject. All of them have a good deal of adult education rather on the lines of the Workers' Educational Association.

The outstanding successes of formal education for citizenship in these five countries are two: the startling result of the Grundtvig educational reforms through the Danish Folk High Schools, which is fully dealt with in Chapter VII —Denmark: A Triumph of Education—and the high standard of education of the present Swedish ministers, which I have just described.

CONCLUSION

Professor Toynbee has suggested that civilisation depends on what he calls " challenge and response ". When the challenge of natural conditions is too severe, man's fortitude breaks down; when things are too easy, men grow lazy and again become degenerate. It is only when conditions are so difficult as to offer a challenge to man's energy, and yet not too difficult, that civilisation progresses.

In the last two generations civilisation has steadily progressed in the three Scandinavian countries. The most difficult conditions were undoubtedly those in agricultural Denmark about 1880, where there was a real danger of collapse; owing to the stimulus of Grundtvig's education, the challenge proved not a curse but a blessing, and the magnificent co-operator-owner system grew out of it. The easiest conditions are those which have been prevailing for the last few years in Sweden, where prosperity has progressed by leaps and bounds. But there are no signs as yet that conditions are so easy as to cause degeneration.

The Scandinavians have proved that they are not dependent on specially favourable conditions; that if left alone in peace and security, they can show the world how to build successful democracies.

The recent history of these five small democracies is a stimulating and encouraging thing, and, particularly, their three outstanding achievements. In Switzerland, the brilliant solution of the minorities problem; the friendly co-operation which has been established between Germans, Frenchmen, and Italians, between Roman Catholics and Protestants: probably the most striking success in history in the art of living together in peace and freedom among peoples of different races, languages, and religions.

Denmark, under the influence of the Danish Folk High Schools, has invented what is nothing less than a new system of agriculture; the co-operator-owner system, perhaps the most scientific and efficient, certainly the most democratic in the world.

Sweden has gone further towards reconciling the interests of town with country, and of capital with labour, than any other nation, and has been the most successful democracy in avoiding the evils of booms and slumps and in working towards the permanent abolition of unemployment. She has an exceptionally wise and able government, and has perhaps the best prospects of any country in the world of establishing something approaching a perfect democracy during the next generation.

This is a book about democracy in peace time; a study of the efforts men are making to overcome the difficulties of modern society when secure from war. A European war might well shatter all these splendid attempts to build a better social order. Even so, it has been worth while studying them. They afford, I hope, definite proof that when the existing tide of barbarism has subsided, men will succeed in building a new and nobler civilisation.

Given peace, it will be a thrilling and inspiriting thing to watch the progress of these fine experiments in the art of living together in security and freedom.